A SOURCEBOOK OF

MANAGEMENT SIMULATIONS

A SOURCEBOOK OF
MANAGEMENT SIMULATIONS

Ken Jones

Kogan Page, London/Nichols Publishing, New York

© Ken Jones, 1989

All rights reserved. No reproduction, copy or transmission of this publication may be made without written permission.

No paragraph of this publication may be reproduced, copied or transmitted save with written permission or in accordance with the provisions of the Copyright Act 1956 (as amended), or under the terms of any licence permitting limited copying issued by the Copyright Licensing Agency, 7 Ridgmount Street, London WC1E 7AE.

> Though this book remains subject to copyright, permission is granted free of charge to photocopy the pages which are required for the simulation to proceed. This may be done for use within the purchasing institution, school or college only.

Any person who does any unauthorised act in relation to this publication may be liable to criminal prosecution and civil claims for damages.

First published in Great Britain in 1989 by Kogan Page Ltd, 120 Pentonville Road, London N1 9JN.

Typeset from author's disks by Saxon Printing Ltd., Derby.
Printed and bound in Great Britain by Billings & Sons Ltd., Worcester

British Library Cataloguing in Publication Data
Jones, Ken, *1923* –
  A sourcebook of management simulations.
  1. Management. Simulation games
  I. Title
  658.4'0353

ISBN 1-85091-890-2

First published in the United States of America in 1989 by Nichols Publishing, an imprint of GP Publishing Inc., PO Box 96, New York, NY 10024

Library of Congress Cataloguing in Publication Data
Jones, Ken, *1923* –
  A sourcebook of management simulations/Ken Jones.
    p.   cm.
  ISBN 0-89397-345-9 : $22.50
  1. Management—Simulation methods.   I. Title
  HD30.26.J66   1989
  658.4'0352—dc19   89-3218
                    CIP

Contents

Acknowledgments	7
PART 1: INTRODUCTION	9
Chapter 1: The scope of the book	11
Management as a verb embracing interactive skills	11
Simulations as distinct from games, exercises and role-plays	13
Professional intent, decision making, communication skills	16
Trainers, teachers, facilitators, participants	20
Chapter 2: How to use the book	26
Hands-on experience	26
The order of presenting the simulations	26
Time, numbers, furniture, facilities, TV studio, photocopying	28
Briefing	30
Action	31
Debriefing	34
Chapter 3: The style of the ten simulations	37
Simplicity of format, subtlety of action	37
Varied, unusual, open ended	39
Participant roles involving managing the event's mechanics	40
Built-in follow-up opportunities	41
PART 2: THE TEN SIMULATIONS	43

1. STOP TALKING – In a company where the trainers talk too much, the executives and trainers meet to plan interactive simulations and exercises for a new training package.
   Skills: technique awareness, authorship, cooperation, assessing, planning   46

2. PAPER LAUNCH – A newspaper is launched amid fierce competition and executives and advertisers of three papers prepare and broadcast their own television commercials.
   Skills: market planning, authorship, publicity, presentation   50

3. CAN WE SAVE LOGO MOTORS? – Executives, consultants, trade unionists and ministers discuss plans to rescue ailing industrial giant.
   Skills: analysing, planning, negotiating, decision making   54

4. OUTERWORLD TRADE – Ministers of the Five Planets introduce interplanetary trade, switch production to the most effective areas, engage in trading negotiations, and are interviewed by interplanetary broadcasters.
   Skills: production decisions, bargaining, trading, interviewing   68

5. PEG SPOTTING – Trainees and assessors at the Ministry of Careers engage in assessment activities for the purpose of fitting people into the jobs most suited for them.
   Skills: personal relationships, flexibility, insights, assessments   84

6. FORT – Teams of architects (2000 years ago) decide on the design of a fort and where it should be built.
   Skills: evaluation, planning, strategy, design, decision making   92

7. LINK MANAGEMENT – Companies competing for a contract for children's entertainment at a chain of hotels are asked to produce plans and manufacture appropriate paper chains on a production line basis and then to present their plans and products effectively and entertainingly to the hotel management.
   Skills: organization, planning, design, manufacture, entertainment   96

8. COMPUTER WORLD – Officials, executives, consultants and a journalist, some with inside knowledge and confidential information about computer software piracy, hacking and espionage, meet in pairs or groups in imaginary locations in pursuit of their own interests.
   Skills: confidentiality, diplomacy, subtlety, investigation, ethics   100

9. ROCK ISLAND – A three-part event in which the participants are in turn citizens, officials, and politicians in a poor country which has suddenly become rich by the discovery of off-shore oil, which ends in party political broadcasts.
   Skills: preferences, planning, analysis, decision making, presentation   106

10. SELLING THE FLAG – Politicians of three parties of a mid-Atlantic country debate proposals to sell the country.
    Skills: evaluating, planning, interviewing, presenting, debating   114

PART 3: BIBLIOGRAPHY   **121**

Acknowledgments

Authors of simulations need people who are willing to try out the prototype versions, and my grateful thanks go to the indispensable one thousand or so trainees, students, trainers and teachers who acted as guinea pigs.

Special thanks go to fellow members of SAGSET – the Society for the Advancement of Games and Simulations in Education and Training – for their helpful comments over the years of development, and in particular to Rod Dawson, senior lecturer at Portsmouth Polytechnic's Department of Management Development, who, in his capacity as calligrapher, kindly produced the 'ancient' script in FORT.

Part One
Introduction

Chapter 1

The scope of the book

Management as a verb embracing interactive skills

In the title of this book 'management' does not mean a collection of managers, but rather what people do when they manage — plan, assess, cooperate, design, negotiate, bargain, organize, analyse, propose, decide, explain, present. In this sense management is a verb covering a wide range of interaction.

Management as an action word is reflected in the roles of the participants. Although some will find themselves in the traditional roles of business managers, there are also roles for trade unionists, workers, consultants, trainers, trainees, advertisers, politicians, civil servants, ministers, journalists, military architects, industrial spies, citizens. Thus, for the purposes of the events, management is not conceived as a sort of exclusive boardroom club but rather as what happens in a series of problematic situations involving roles which call for management in one form or another.

A simulation in this book is also a verb — it is interaction. So although one might say 'This book contains ten simulations' it is more accurate to say 'This book contains the materials for ten simulations'. In this sense simulations are things that occur — they are not materials, nor aims, nor 'representations'.

It may seem strange to dissociate 'simulations' from 'representations' since most authors define a simulation as a representation of reality. This is fine if one is talking about wind tunnels, or maps, or TV graphics showing the separation stages of a space rocket. But if the context is interactive events then to envisage it as a representation is to miss the whole point. For example, an instructor, having observed a management simulation, might say 'That was an excellent representation of a boardroom discussion — you mirrored reality very well, you imitated and simulated the atmosphere' to which the ex-participants might reply 'We were not representing, mirroring, imitating or simulating, we were fighting to save our company'.

The only real way to understand a simulation is to see it from the inside — from the viewpoint of the participants who are doing the job.

From their point of view they are not imitators, or modellers, or representers. If, during the event, they think 'I am in a simulation' or 'What will the instructor say if I do such and such?' then they are not thinking with professional intent, they are not properly in their roles, and the event is not a genuine simulation. If a role card says 'You are a journalist...' it is also saying 'You are not a trainee, student, pupil, learner, imitator, player, gamester, play-actor, clown ...'

In the debriefing after the event the participants must be able to give professional reasons for their behaviour — 'I did it because I wished to make Logo Motors more efficient' or 'I asked provocative questions because tough questions make good television'. If ex-participants say 'I behaved like that because I was imitating a manager I saw on television last night' or 'I asked those questions because I thought I'd have a bit of fun' then for those persons the event was not a simulation. Simulations are about professional intent, participant autonomy, and the right to make mistakes. Two points follow from this.

First, a simulation, by definition, must be a non-taught event. Whatever the ultimate aims of the facilitator (to convey information, reproduce the real world, give practice in management skills) a simulation can never be a guided exercise or a training session since this would deny participant autonomy and preclude role acceptance.

Secondly, from the point of view of the participants a simulation is real, not pretend. There is real analysis not simulated analysis. There are real discussions, real interviews, real decisions — not mimicry. The only simulated aspect is the environment.

The environment must be simulated otherwise the event is not a simulation, it is real. Without a simulated environment there are no roles since the jobs are real with real consequences and affect real outsiders. It is no longer isolated and safe. If a group of students or trainees engages in a mini enterprise then the money will be real and there could even be real fraud or a real visit from a government inspector. If the group produces a newspaper for their college or company then not only will there be real readers there could be a real writ complaining of libel. As seen from the point of view of the participants a simulation can be defined as:

> A non-taught event in which the participants have sufficient information to enable them to behave with professional intent according to their roles.

Recent years have seen a large increase in the use of the simulation technique. It is now a respectable and usually indispensable aspect of training in business and industry, in teaching foreign languages, in training trainers and teachers, and in general use in British secondary schools and colleges. So whereas a few years ago the almost inevitable

The scope of the book 13

first question was 'What is a simulation?' the question today is 'How can we use simulations more effectively'. However 'What is a simulation?' is still an important question, since misconceptions abound, and these lead to muddled events.

Simulations as distinct from games, exercises and role-play

This section is probably the most important in the Introduction since by far the most common cause of failure of simulations is muddled terminology. This leads to mistaken expectations which in turn leads to what I term ambivalents. Ambivalents are events which involve techniques that are not only different but are incompatible.

To avoid ambivalents it is important for the terminology and the expectations to match the technique. Even if the terminology is right this may not be enough if there already exist powerful mistaken expectations — as when a drama class expects a drama instead of a simulation, or when trainees have already played a game or two on the course and expect more of the same. Before running any of these ten simulations it is advisable for facilitators to watch out for signs that an ambivalent may occur — which usually means sensitivity to chance remarks like 'Are we playing a game this afternoon?'

Mistaken expectations occur because many authors use the labels interchangeably. What is referred to as a 'game' in the first sentence becomes a 'simulation' in the second, an 'exercise' in the third, and 'role-play' later on. Some authors seek to escape by inventing compound terms — simulation–game, simulation–exercise, role-play–exercise, gaming–exercise. These terms fudge, not clarify, and make matters worse by increasing the number of interchangeable labels. To say 'This is a simulation–game which involves a role-play–exercise' is like saying 'This is a poetry–novel which involves a screwdriver–chisel'. The concepts are incompatible; they are contradictions in terms.

A simple way for facilitators to escape from the muddled labels is to change the basis of categorization. Instead of thinking about the materials, rules, or aims it makes sense to classify according to what goes on in the minds of the participants — the answers to the questions 'Who am I supposed to be?', 'What am I supposed to do?'

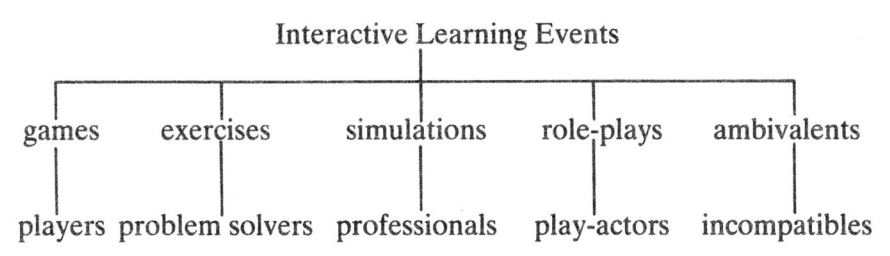

```
                    Interactive Learning Events
    ┌───────────┬───────────┬───────────┬───────────┐
  games     exercises   simulations  role-plays  ambivalents
    │           │           │           │           │
 players  problem solvers professionals play-actors incompatibles
```

The unique nature of the simulation technique becomes clearer when comparing it with other techniques as seen from the inside.

Games

A game is a magic kingdom isolated by its own rules from real world considerations and ethics. In Monopoly no one will say 'It is unethical to knock down all those houses in order to build hotels', or 'I shall refer that to the Monopolies Commission'. If, in football or chess or bridge, a player goes on strike then it is not an event within the game, it is the abandonment of the game. Similarly, cheating is not play, it is a breach of the rules and by definition it cannot be part of the game. If a player says 'You are cheating' then both the alleged cheating and the accusation itself are events outside the magic kingdom. However, in a simulation participants can go on strike or cheat or lie or steal and remain within the event, providing they are behaving with professional intent. It is up to them to face the consequences of what they did within the event itself and in the debriefing afterwards.

In games there is only one role — that of player — and it is the duty of players to try to win while conforming to the rules and the concept of fair play which is an inherent aspect of the rules. Games must always be competitive events whereas simulations, role-plays and exercises are often cooperative events. The outcome of a game cannot be a matter of opinion, it cannot be open ended. There must be a scoring mechanism to determine who has won and who has lost.

Another distinguishing feature is that a game ends with the final score. That is the bottom line. A successful bluff, provided that it is obtained by fair play, requires no justification other than its own success. In a simulation, on the other hand, a successful (or failed) bluff can be criticized both during the event and in the debriefing in relation to its possible effect on the hypothetical future. The question might be 'When you were bluffing did you consider the future effect it might have on both your own reputation and the reputation of your company?'

Exercises

The one clear difference between exercises and simulations is that in an exercise the participants have no roles. They remain themselves — conference goers, trainees, executives, pupils, students. The ideal state of mind of a participant in an exercise is that of objectivity and impartiality. As seen from the inside the participant is a problem solver, a discusser, a puzzler, an analyser, a decision maker.

Unlike a game the participants are not trying to win — they are trying to solve a problem. In the debriefing the key question is not likely to be 'Who won?', but 'How efficient were you?' Exercises, unlike games, can be cooperative and open ended. If the exercise takes the form of a case study then it can embrace all the relevant aspects of the real world — ethics, laws, institutions — something which is impossible in a game.

Role-plays
Role-plays are episodic and brief. They can be functional, in which case the word 'play' is inappropriate, or they can involve play-acting. Functional role-play, if it has sufficient facts to allow professional intent, is really a short simulation. The play-acting type of role-play is really a miniature informal drama.

Since both the functional and play-acting types of role-play rarely have enough facts to allow the participants to behave with professional intent the participants have to take on a hidden secondary role, that of author, and invent most of the key facts for themselves. Imagine that the facilitator sets up a functional role-play with the instructions: 'You are the customer returning a damaged umbrella, and you are the shop assistant and you stand behind that table which is the counter. Carry on.' The following dialogue might occur:

Customer (in role)	I'm returning this umbrella.
Shop assistant (in role)	How did it break?
Customer (switching to author role)	It came to pieces in my hand.

If the author/facilitator injects personality adjectives ('angry' customer, 'irritable' shop assistant) then the participants have to invent the emotions as well as the facts. If the facilitator requires the participants to behave with professional intent and at the same time hands out a role card which says 'angry customer' then cross purposes occur. The following exchanges might take place in the debriefing:

Facilitator: Why did you shout at the shop assistant? Was that the most efficient way of obtaining a refund?
Ex-participant: I was not trying to be efficient or obtain a refund, I was play-acting the emotion of anger.

Role-plays are often (although not always) conducted in a fish-bowl format surrounded by an audience which could either be asked to observe silently or to make comments at suitable points in the action. Fish-bowls are a format of the theatre, a round stage. The audience is an extra environment, a real environment of eyes looking and minds appraising, an environment of coughs, gasps, laughs, remarks, mutterings, silences. This extra and real environment can be part of the play-acting technique, but it is inconsistent with the simulation technique since the audience makes it difficult if not impossible to behave with professional intent.

Ambivalents

Many authors are muddled about techniques so it is not surprising that the materials are often inconsistent. The facilitator's notes might say 'The aim of this simulation is to develop managerial skills' while the role cards are too instructional ('The plan you must put forward is...') or are written in a way which invites play-acting ('You are a tough boss...').

A consequence of muddled materials and interchangeable labels is that facilitators often unwittingly give self-contradictory briefings. To say 'In this game you will be engaged in a business simulation which is an exercise in which you role-play the function of managers' will not provide the participants with a clear idea about who they are supposed to be and what they are supposed to do and why. If all participants treat it as a simulation then that is what it is. If some behave one way while others behave another way then it is an ambivalent and dissatisfaction is high on the agenda. The conceptual muddle not only produces damaged events it also stands in the way of diagnosing the cause of the damage.

The most common type of interactive learning event is probably an ambivalent and the reason why this is not generally recognized is because ambivalents generate their own smoke screens. Plenty of examples of ambivalents and smoke are given elsewhere (Jones 1988a p 127-43). Briefly, an ambivalent is usually characterized by:

1. the facilitator being surprised at the emotion during the event;
2. lack of any plausible explanation;
3. the facilitator tends to blame the participants;
4. the participants tend to blame each other;
5. important aspects 'do not show up in the research results'.

Even if people are too polite to voice their displeasure there can be an undercurrent of bewilderment and hurt feelings which can lead to person A being reluctant to sit next to B in the canteen, and for C to criticize D's behaviour when describing the event to friend Z.

For a facilitator to be hit by an ambivalent can be similar to receiving an unexpected blow on the head — it is a shock, it is unpleasant, and it bewilders.

Professional intent, decision making, communication skills

Professional intent

Professional intent does not imply professional expertise, and in most simulations that are used in education and training the participants are not experts. The word 'intent' indicates that what matters is not expertise but willingness to try to do the job. The essential requirement is that participants accept the responsibilities of their roles and do the best they can in the situations in which they find themselves. The word 'professional' is intended to cover any function requiring some form of managerial skills. For example, at the start of ROCK ISLAND the participants are citizens who have to take account of the interests of their families and plan accordingly.

The main enemy of professional intent is a gaming attitude. At this point it may be worth examining why it is that American literature on management and education is so hooked on the word 'game'. This is not really a digression since this literature has a powerful influence outside the United States and an examination helps to clarify the issues.

As argued elsewhere (Jones 1988a, 1988b) national cultures influence the categorization of interactive learning events and in the United States there is a much closer link between professional intent and the concept of a game than in Britain or most other countries. For one thing, American education and training are very similar to games in the sense that they tend to be highly competitive. Since the funding of schools, colleges and training centres in the United States usually depends on results there is a strong inclination to seek to justify the projects by frequent testing and grading based on objective tests of fact learning. As with games, American education and training is out to win. By contrast, British education and training is more concerned with the process than with the product.

As well as American education having affinities to games, American football and baseball have affinities to education and training. Both are more intellectual than their counterparts of soccer or cricket. In American football, but not in English football or English rugby, teams have the right to suspend the game for a discussion of strategies. Teams of any importance in American college or professional football have books of dozens of 'plays' which are far more precise (and academic) than anything used in strategy discussions in traditional British sports. In baseball there is plenty of time between pitches for communicating plans. Television close-ups have revealed the game to be full of secret signals — twitches, yawns, shrugs, foot tappings — passing between coaches, pitchers, catchers and fielders about the type of pitch to be thrown next. Although in traditional British sports there are signals between the coaches and the players and between the players themselves this is nothing compared with the scientific planning which goes on in American football and baseball.

As well as time for planning there is also the possession factor. In American football the team at the line of scrimmage is in possession of the ball. Thus, the release of the ball can be planned with considerable accuracy, far more so than in the case of a ball placed in the middle of a rugby scrum. Similarly, in baseball the act of throwing allows for more control over the trajectory and the arrival point than the act of bowling in cricket. In the United States, therefore, there is much in common between games, management and education.

Although all cultures use gaming terminology in some managerial or political situations this seems to be far more prevalent in the United States than elsewhere. In America the phrase 'Let's have a game plan' has more analytical and professional implications than if used in Britain where it would probably be taken to mean 'Let's have an informal chat about what to do next'. In Britain 'Let's make a play' is not a phrase normally used and would probably mean 'Let's do something' or possibly 'Let's make a play for the girls'. In the United States it has considerable managerial and scientific connotations. It implies professional intent.

In Britain the word 'exercise' is frequently used as a label to cover all interactive events, and is usually taken to imply professional intent. A notable exception is in business management training where there has been a tendency to follow American terminology and refer to 'business games' and 'management games.' However, similar interactive events for the lower paid staff are usually called exercises. Thus, intentionally or not, the label 'game' has an elitist implication in management and may convey the coded meaning 'We know it is not really a game, but it shows that we in management are laid back, informal, humorous, self-deprecating.' However, once it is acknowledged that a simulation is not a game it is inefficient and dangerous to use the label. Even in American business and education the use of gaming terminology is something of an own goal, particularly when trying to inform the public (shareholders, customers, parents) what is going on. In common parlance games are the things that are sold in games shops, so the word carries with it associations of entertainment and amusement involving a magic kingdom with only tenuous links with the world of real business, real management, real education. Large organizations — business, government, academic circles, the armed forces — are using more professional labels.

On both sides of the Atlantic the most tenacious users of the misnomer 'game' are the media. The label makes for snappy headlines — in newspapers, in film titles, and on radio and television. Also it can have a smear effect — 'Costly government war games', 'Games instead of lessons at XYZ school'. By the time the professionals have explained 'These are not really games but are serious simulations for education and training' the story is old, and no one wants to hear boring academic explanations anyway.

Decision making

Simulations, unlike discussions, must involve decision making about doing something, or not doing something. Action must be under consideration as the outcome of the decision making. It may also be part of the decision making process itself. The participants could analyse the problem, do research, make statements, give news conferences, interview, plan, recommend, write reports, hold protest meetings, negotiate contracts, deal with personnel problems. So long as a decision is related to action it does not have to be a clear-cut directive, nor need it be an agreement. 'We cannot decide on doing A or B until we obtain more facts' is a decision, it contains the concept of doing. If the outcome is 'We could not agree on what to do' then this is still a decision in two ways. First, people have made individual decisions relating to action, albeit not implemented, and secondly they have jointly decided against imposing one particular decision on the rest by means of voting or by dictatorship. Decisions in the sense used in this book relate to action, not to the wording of some document. Even passive resistance by minority voters would be classified as a decision — namely the decision to withdraw cooperation.

One implication of decision making as part of the simulation technique is that the participants must have the power to make decisions on their own, however ill-considered, disorganized, or just plain stupid such decisions might be. So if the participants are not used to having professional responsibilities and are conditioned to expect instructional methods then it can be necessary to explain that a simulation is not a rehearsed event or a guided exercise. It is useful to explain that mistakes are not only inevitable they are to be welcomed, since perhaps the most effective learning of all is when people learn from their mistakes. However, it is often true that such explanations in the briefing of their first simulation have little or no effect, so it is sometimes better to forget the preliminary chat and let them learn from hands-on experience.

The essential and necessary implication of simulations is that the task is doing, not learning. Of course, people learn from doing, but the documents and the motives are intended for action. A document is not there to be learned, it is there to be used. Decision making is a process, not a conclusion. The aim of the simulations in this book is not to produce a pile of 'right' decisions, it is to learn from experience how to make decisions effectively. These simulations necessarily involve trial and error, and errors are a highly efficient way of learning.

Communication skills
All ten simulations are designed to be highly interactive, with an absence of part time or passive roles. Communication between participants is essential if they are to behave effectively.

In all the simulations there are plenty of opportunities for oral communication — discussing, arguing, persuading, stating a case, interviewing, explaining, presenting. There are also opportunities for written communications — notes, memos, diagrams, maps. Indeed, the use made of scrap paper is often a measure of professionalism in these simulations. Those participants who do not jot down ideas, or make notes of what others say, or draw diagrams to assist their own thinking are often (but not always) those who are operating well below the level of their own potential and contributing least to effective communication.

A characteristic of communication in simulations is reality of function. The participants focus on the job itself — the duties, responsibilities, opportunities — and how to communicate effectively. By contrast, one of the problems with the alternative technique of play-acting is that a good performance often becomes more important than the effective communication of ideas, in which case *how* something is said can become more important than *what* is said. Also, play-acting can cause stage fright. Although the extraverts enjoy themselves the shy actors often retreat ever further into the background. In simulations, on the other hand, the job-related duties help shy participants to concentrate on their responsibilities to others and forget their personal fears.

This is not to argue that simulations never involve anything dramatic or theatrical, only to emphasize that in the context of communication skills and managerial efficiency any dramatic remarks or gestures must be subservient to the main aims; otherwise the event becomes an informal drama or an ambivalent.

As indicated already, a major cause of failure in running non-taught interactive learning events is incompatible techniques introduced inadvertently by the facilitator. Ambivalents are undesirable not least because they contaminate the lines of communication between people. In ambivalents the participants fly off at cross purposes. Because of basic misunderstandings about roles and motives various remarks, gestures and criticisms occur which are inappropriate and hurtful. Once the participants become used to simulations as simulations (not thinking about them as games or exercises) then the communication will become more effective and misunderstandings, annoyances, and even anger due to technique confusion will diminish.

Trainers, teachers, facilitators, participants

The ten simulations have been tried out in a variety of situations — in management courses, in business studies in colleges of further education, in the teaching of English as a foreign language, in teacher education, and in the upper levels of secondary schools. There are plenty of examples which confirm what others have found with open ended simulations — that it is unsafe to pre-judge people's ability in such events on the basis of age, or academic ability, or managerial status, or examination results, or race, or gender.

The scope of the book 21

This section contains a series of examples of the need to keep an open mind. Observations about what does happen in simulations are more valuable than assumptions about what is supposed to happen. The theme running through the whole of this section is that people should be treated like human beings.

Young professionals
Although some of the language in the simulation documents in this book is sophisticated, the actual basic tasks are relatively simple. For a teacher or instructor to say 'These are unsuitable for my group because they have had no experience of simulations' is to forget childhood. Very young children devise simulations spontaneously — doctors and patients, goodies and baddies. The child in the role of doctor might say 'Where does it hurt?' and express sympathy. This is a completely different technique from play-acting, as when a child might imitate the actions of a doctor using a stethoscope but is unaware of the purpose of the instrument. The fact that adults would call both the above examples 'play' shows how easy it is to confuse the professionalism of the first example with the mimicry of the second.

There is evidence that 11-year-olds are actually better than 14-year-olds at simulations (Jones 1987a, p 99). The younger children often sit in a group and work as a group, whereas the older children often tend to sit together but work as individuals with little or no communication. One teacher, disappointed by seeing the inefficiency of her 14-year-olds compared with witnessing the same simulation run earlier with a class of 11-year-olds said 'We've unabled them'. The explanation given by the teacher was that 11-year-olds were closer than 14-year-olds to primary school experiences where they had professional responsibilities — experimenters, architects, sales people, customers, builders, designers, mothers and fathers in the Wendy House.

Obviously, young children do not show the sophistication of adults when participating in simulations, and the briefing of the events at this level should take this into account. However, it is not always the case that adults are more efficient than children. LINK MANAGEMENT was run in a secondary school with 13-year-olds and later with a group of teachers at the school. During the debriefing of the teachers the class teacher of the 13-year-olds produced the actual links made by the children. Much to the surprise of the teachers these links were more imaginative and entertaining than those produced by the teachers and therefore the young chain-makers were more efficient in the context — that of securing a contract.

Something similar occurred with COMPUTER WORLD regarding children and trainers. When the event was run with 15-year-old (male) students at a secondary school in a deprived area of London several participants spontaneously bought from A and sold to B, thus making a considerable profit. When a group of instructors in the training department of a large industrial company tried out COMPUTER WORLD they traded with sophistication but everyone either bought or sold, and no participant did both, presumably because it did not occur to them to do so. Their roles had mentioned that there was a need to buy (or sell) and they did no more than that, thus lacking the managerial enterprise of several of the 15-year-olds.

The revelation value of simulations
It can be seen from the above examples that quite apart from the education and training benefits of simulations they also have the valuable capacity of revelation. Although it may at times be an unpleasant shock to discover that assumptions are incorrect, it is usually a salutary experience. The revelations are not simply related to individual participants, but to the effectiveness of the training course, the assumptions behind the examination results, the stereotypes which deceive and corrupt the analysis.

At a conference of SAGSET (Society for the Advancement of Games and Simulations in Education and Training) a lecturer described how he had run a simulation on a management course at a polytechnic in which teams representing competing companies engaged in trading and had to draw up balance sheets for their firms. Before the event everyone thought there would be no problem with the balance sheets since the students had successfully passed their examinations covering that topic. 'We did that last year' was how they put it. Then came the nasty shock — the simulation revealed that the students were unable to cope with the task of drawing up their balance sheets. They had satisfied the examiners that they could do balance sheets in theory, but they had not been tested to see if they could do so in practice. The simulation revealed the truth behind the pass marks.

In most countries students go into the world of work believing that their examination successes will help them not only to get a job but also to do a job. It is an assumption which is usually shared by their teachers and by business management. Consequently it is usually with surprise and disappointment in their voices that managers and trainers complain that school leavers 'Are not very good at thinking for themselves' and 'They show no initiative and can't cope with simple jobs'. The bewilderment may be due to an attitude of mind which assumes that education is like some people's attitude to quality control — 'Never mind how it was made, just let's see if it passes the test at the end of the line.' It is an attitude which sees education and business in terms of products rather than processes.

In Britain the position regarding school leavers is in a process of favourable change. Various educational initiatives in the late 1980s have had a revolutionary effect, particularly the introduction of the General Certificate of Secondary Education which includes active learning, group work, and compulsory oral assessment in the English examinations. The GCSE examination requirement transformed classroom practices almost overnight. Her Majesty's Inspectors (1988) reported a dramatic increase in the effectiveness of lessons. HMI said: 'The GCSE has played a part in raising expectations. Most teachers appear to have become more aware of what pupils are capable of achieving.'

American schools versus American culture
In the United States the students continue to receive a heavy diet of instructional teaching. The aim seems to be to produce diligent hermits. Yet this system of step-by-step learning and frequent testing of factual knowledge has come under intense criticism from American educationalists. For examples see John Goodlad (1984) regarding education and Leo Ruth and Sandra Murphy (1988) regarding assessment. In the United States there are significant new trends which emphasize group learning and human interaction. At the University of California at Berkeley there are at least three separate projects which do this. One is the Bay Area Writing Project which uses imaginative stimuli for group work. The staff on the Project deplore the fact that standardized writing tests involve no writing, only marking boxes in the multiple choice format. Another group-based project (in mathematics) is the EQUALS Program dealing with equal opportunities for girls, which uses exercises and simulations. The third is an advanced mathematics course based on workshops and group activities instead of the usual lectures and individualized study. All three projects have yielded impressive results.

Despite cowboy films it is a mistake to think that American culture is typified by the individualism of the lone ranger, and that schools are merely reflecting the mainstream American culture. On the contrary, the American pioneers succeeded by group efforts, and American culture is basically a community culture, and it is democratic. By contrast, those educational and training establishments which are dominated by instructional methods often unwittingly teach all concerned that pupils/students/trainees have second class status. But with simulations the technique itself demands equal respect for facilitator and participants alike. The bestowal of participant autonomy is an implicit statement of human values — of respect, and of trust.

Gender and race
A mismatch between the myth and the reality can be caused by thinking in stereotypes, as frequently occurs regarding gender and race. On the question of gender it is sometimes assumed by instructors and teachers

that females are not as forthcoming as males, that they are less willing to answer questions put by the instructor, that in group work they often take a back seat (or get pushed aside by the males) and that generally speaking they are more amenable and compliant than males. What is rarely appreciated is that the conclusion is heavily dependent on the circumstances of instructional methodology. If the methodology is changed to simulations then surprises occur. Instructors and teachers are often quite astonished that the participants are not conforming to their gender stereotype. 'I'm surprised that Amanda spoke up like she did' is the sort of remark which is often heard. It reveals not only something about Amanda, but also something about the instructor's previous assumptions and assessments. Nor is the surprise limited to the instructors; it can be general throughout the group, particularly by the males who are sometimes shocked (and usually pleased) that the females are asserting themselves.

The same situation can occur with race. The received opinion is that blacks do not do as well as whites in educational situations. Again this ignores the influence of instructional methodology in narrowing human behaviour to silent passive individualistic learning. Simulations, on the other hand, involve sound and people, and equal opportunities. Instead of the background thought 'Me, I'm black (Asian, white, male, female, student, etc) and my job is to receive and learn instructions' it is 'Me, I'm a manager and my job is to manage'. There is a world of difference between the two attitudes.

As mentioned elsewhere (Jones 1987a; p 98) there is evidence that in open-ended simulations West Indians on the whole are not only as good as whites, but they are more efficient. On the whole (there are significant exceptions) the West Indians are more imaginative and more effective in their arguments and presentations. For example, in one simulation where they had to read their reports aloud to other participants the West Indians would tend to look up, obtaining eye contact, improvising and receiving feedback, whereas white children tended to put their heads down and read (mumble) everything they had written word for word. The reason for this difference is presumably the importance of the oral tradition and group activities in West Indian culture compared with the predominance of the written word and solitary work in the white culture. In the United States similar conclusions have been reached about the effective oral culture of blacks. See particularly Labov (1972).

Human values and equal opportunities
Regarding specific human values, most simulations, and certainly the ten in this book, favour equal opportunities. The participants work in groups based on jobs, and since the allocation of roles is (or should be)

at random there is no favouritism and no cliques. This contrasts with walking into a classroom or training centre and finding that the females are all sitting at one table while all the males are at another, or that the students are seated in self-segregated groupings according to race. The integration of individuals in simulations is far more effective than giving lectures about the evils of discrimination while at the same time allowing the trainees to practise their own form of segregation and discrimination typified by possessive attitudes towards my chair, my friends, my group. Segregation and discrimination based on race, gender or anything else is not only unfair, it is inefficient. It is a management problem — management at all levels, including classroom management. It is within the province of facilitators and participants to do something about it.

Chapter 2

How to use the book

Hands-on experience

Before running any of the ten simulations it is important for facilitators to have hands-on experience. It is not enough just to read the documents.

At the very least the facilitator should mentally run through the event in role, and switch roles to see what could be said or done in relation to what some other participant says or does. Better still is to ask a few friends or colleagues to spend 10 or 20 minutes running through at least part of the event so that the actual words will be spoken out loud. These words should be in the first person. Instead of talking hypothetically — 'If I was an executive in STOP TALKING I would explain the situation to the trainers' — it is far better to address the others directly — 'Thank you very much for meeting with us — and for the coffee. It's very good. As you know we've just had a report from the firm of consultants and I have here Appendix C of their report which deals with Staff Training....' It does not matter whether the spoken words are sophisticated or inept, what matters is that they should be real, direct, first hand. This is necessary in order to get inside the event, to meet the people and not just the paper.

The reason for trial runs is not only to see what might happen, but also to provide nitty gritty evidence about such things as how long the event might last, what facilities might be provided, and the sort of issues that could be raised, not only in the action but also in the debriefing. This preliminary run provides a participant's eye view of the challenges and opportunities, a view which is often very different from that of an instructor who merely reads the documents. Just how long and thorough a trial run should be depends largely on the experience of the facilitator in using simulations.

The order of presenting the simulations

The ten simulations can be run in any order, depending on the aims of the facilitator and the nature of the course. For example, within the

How to use the book 27

overall concept of managing they could be grouped according to subject areas, or skills.

Economics:	CAN WE SAVE LOGO MOTORS? OUTERWORLD TRADE LINK MANAGEMENT ROCK ISLAND
Design:	STOP TALKING PAPER LAUNCH PEG SPOTTING FORT LINK MANAGEMENT
Politics:	OUTERWORLD TRADE ROCK ISLAND SELLING THE FLAG
Media:	PAPER LAUNCH OUTERWORLD TRADE COMPUTER WORLD ROCK ISLAND
Staff:	STOP TALKING PEG SPOTTING LINK MANAGEMENT

The order in which they are presented in this book is not according to subject. The reason for this is to provide contrasts, to encourage innovation, and to pay homage to the idea that the capacity to cope with new situations is a key quality in management.

However, the order is not entirely random, and there are reasons why STOP TALKING and PAPER LAUNCH are the first two simulations in the collection.

STOP TALKING is first because it is about training for management, and because it highlights the concept of interactive learning. It involves the participants in designing and evaluating simulations and exercises.

- The hands-on experience of design can in itself do a great deal to justify the methodology. Once people have to design something for themselves then it becomes more personal and more pertinent.
- The clarification of the concept of the different techniques should facilitate effective behaviour in future simulations and avoid ambivalents.
- Some of the outlines for exercises and simulations could be worthy of development and become part of the training course. Having created the outlines the participants might wish to see them used, thus indirectly extending the interaction between the facilitator, the participants, and the course itself.

28 *Introduction*

PAPER LAUNCH is given second place because it combines interest in the media with creativity. It works well not only in top-level management courses but also with 14 year-olds in secondary schools, and in courses for the teaching of English as a foreign language. In non-management courses it could well be used as the first simulation because:

- Everyone is aware of newspapers and the differences between the popular press and quality papers.
- The format of a television advertisement is familiar and opens the door to a variety of important skills — creative presentation, explanation, promotion.
- Important side-issues are likely to arise: ethical standards, the law of libel, marketing concepts.
- Personal qualities are influential — a sense of humour, artistic touches, creativity, organizational ability.

Depending on the nature of the course it is often valuable to negotiate the order of presentation with the students/trainees. This could be either as a general discussion in which the facilitator presents the outline of the simulations, or selecting a small sub-committee of trainees (sworn to secrecy) who could appraise the materials and perhaps themselves take over the running of the event(s).

Time, numbers, furniture, facilities, TV studio, photocopying

The information and advice in this section is supplemented by the Facilitator's Notes for the individual simulations.

Time

For all ten simulations the average time required is between one and three hours, including briefing and debriefing. In all the events it is possible to adjourn the activity on a plausible pretext until a later session. Once the participants get used to the format then the time spent on briefing and the delays in the participants getting started during the first part of the action will be reduced. There can also be a trade-off between facilitator time and participant time. If the participants organize the events themselves then the facilitator can have more time for observation and assessment.

Numbers

The minimum number for each of the simulations is about eight. There is no maximum number: that depends on the size of the room(s) available, since with dozens (or hundreds) of participants the events can be run in parallel.

How to use the book 29

Furniture
The importance of furniture is considerable. It is highly desirable that furniture — tables, desks, chairs, flip-charts — should be movable. Huge conference tables or chairs nailed to the floor do not rule out the use of these simulations but they make it more difficult to organize the events with efficiency and plausibility. Furniture may need to be moved not only for the start of the simulation but also during the event itself to take account of some change in the activities — news conferences, small groups becoming large groups or vice versa, broadcasts, debates, announcements. Participants should be encouraged to improvise (and move) the furniture according to changes in context.

Facilities
The basic facilities for the simulations are the photocopied documents, pens and paper for making notes, plus the occasional use of such items as glue, scissors, paper clips. Most of the simulations can be enhanced by information technology. If the organization has word processors, desktop publishers, video cameras, telephones, pocket calculators, flip charts, chalkboards, overhead projectors, photocopiers and an art department, then with a little forethought these can be used to increase efficient interaction and add the realism of modern management. However, it is important not to use the technology for its own sake and to avoid the danger of being overwhelmed by it. The equipment should help the action not hinder it. It should increase group cooperation and not result in a line of individuals working away at their computers.

The technology should be built into the events. For example, the video camera operator should be given a role — part of the broadcasting team in OUTERWORLD TRADE or part of the Hotel group's assessment facilities in LINK MANAGEMENT.

Depending on the simulation there are often little touches which can increase realism and make the job easier. For example, clipboards could be given to the executives in STOP TALKING, PAPER LAUNCH and LINK MANAGEMENT, to the assessors in PEG SPOTTING, and to anyone in the role of journalist.

There are also what might be called negative facilities — those which impede the action. These consist mainly of personal clobber — outdoor clothing, lunch boxes, bags, headsets, chemistry homework — anything inappropriate for the occasion. Such items should be placed on a side table or anywhere else that is out of the way so that they do not interfere with the participants mentally accepting their roles.

TV studio
Several of the simulations require a television studio. In practice the studio can be entirely imaginary — just a few chairs or whatever

furniture is appropriate for that particular transmission. If a proper studio is available then there should be no technical problems, but when video cameras and tape recorders are imported into a classroom or training centre there can be several problems with the acoustics. The walls may be bare and have a disagreeable echo effect, there could be the hum of air conditioners, clatter from corridors, and noises from neighbouring rooms. One way of minimizing the interference when using a tape recorder is to place a chair on a table with a coat over the back of the chair and the microphone on the seat of the chair. Placing the chair so that the coat is between the microphone and the major source of external noise will help the quality of the recording. Another simple way to improve recordings is to lower the recording level on the machine and request that the broadcasters move closer to the microphone when it is their turn to speak.

Photocopying
All rights are reserved and this book remains subject to copyright, but permission is granted to photocopy free of charge the Notes for Participants and the documents for participants for use within the training centre, college or school.

The number of photocopies required depends on participant need. It is not a matter of saying 'We'll have 20 copies of everything'. The number of Notes for Participants could equal the number taking part, whereas a confidential document might need only one or two copies.

The latest generation of photocopiers can reduce or increase the size of the documents and although the documents in this book are adequate in size they could be reduced or made larger for reasons of administrative convenience. In some cases, such as a document representing a list of official statistics or the page of a newspaper, the size could be increased to enhance realism.

Briefing

The main purpose of the briefing is to explain the mechanics of the event, to allocate roles, to fix time limits (or approximate time limits), and to explain the facilities available. Sometimes it is a good idea to allocate roles and divide into groups before dealing with what is said in the Notes for Participants. As recommended earlier, the roles should be allocated at random. One way is write the roles on the back of the Notes for Participants and then place them face up and ask the participants to pick their own. Dividing into groups before discussing the Notes for Participants allows people to get into role mentally and concentrate on those parts of the briefing which especially concern them rather than trying to 'learn' the whole thing. If the facilitator feels that a particular individual would be unable to cope with a particular role (say that of journalist) then two people could be allocated at random to the role and could help each other. It might be better still to take the chance that a 'weak' participant gets a key role since predictions about participant inadequacies are often wide of the mark, and facilitators are often surprised how well certain individuals cope with simulations.

For participants who are not used to simulations the first briefing is likely to be fraught with unnecessary anxieties and the facilitator can take this into account. However, this should be in the form of sympathy and understanding, not lengthy explanations. There is a good case for getting nervous participants into the action as quickly as possible. Once they experience simulations then confidence increases.

Inexperienced facilitators sometimes use the briefing to give examples and advice on policy matters in order to improve the 'quality' of the event and ensure 'success'. This is a mistake of category. Policy making is for the participants, and should not be preempted by clever hints from the facilitator. What is stated in Notes for Participants is sufficient in almost all cases. An illustration of what not to do is for a facilitator to speculate about (or invite a discussion on) the meaning of the final sentence in Appendix C in STOP TALKING:

> From the point of view of the executives the activity is likely to reveal more than just the outlines of simulations and exercises.

For the facilitator to say 'That sentence might mean that the executives could use the event to assess the trainers for the vacant post of head of staff training' is not only to remove a problem which is there to be tackled, it seriously erodes participant authority, and it reflects adversely on the professionalism of the facilitator.

Participants do not mind getting it wrong; they do mind having their problem pre-preempted by over-protective (and perhaps egotistic) facilitators. A facilitator should not be an instructor in disguise.

Special care should be taken not to convey additional facts. In COMPUTER WORLD the journalist has devised a smart virus. For the facilitator to mention the concept of a smart virus in the briefing not only reveals something which the participants can find out for themselves in conversation with the journalist but alerts the participants to the probability that one of their number does have a smart virus on offer.

To sum up. The briefing should be brief. It should not include helpful hints about policy matters, nor should it attempt to coach. It should not include discussion of the working documents since these exist only in the action part of the simulation. The main purpose of the briefing is to announce (and discuss) the mechanics of the event, the facilities, and the time limits.

Action

At least nine times out of ten the simulations will run themselves and the facilitator will have no need to interfere. Assuming the briefing was reasonably adequate then the participants will have no need to ask questions about the mechanics of the event, and will know enough about the nature of the simulation technique not to seek advice from the facilitator on policy decisions nor ask for helpful hints.

The facilitator should aim to be invisible, or at least impassive. This low profile is an excellent position to observe and assess what happens. During the debriefing it is usually more effective to quote actual examples rather than generalize. People's words are their personal investments. For the facilitator to say 'The boss said it was easy' is not as effective as 'The boss said "It's a piece of cake"'. Remembering the actual words also makes the participants accept the ownership of their own views.

The Notes for Participants states that the participants can do anything they are not told not to do, providing they accept their roles and responsibilities. This professional power means that the facilitator should be prepared for events to take one or two unexpected turns. However, observation of what is said and done is likely to give advance warning of what might occur, and will probably raise the question of the mechanics of the event. 'We want to give a news conference' is the sort of initiative which could happen unexpectedly. The facilitator can then given an instantaneous ruling, or suspend the activity to discuss details of any new arrangements including the timing of the news conference and its location.

The essential proviso to the powers of the participants — accepting professional responsibilities — has the practical effect of placing the facilitator in charge of the authorship of the simulated environment. The participants can order a strike, or call for a day of prayer, or issue the orders to double production, or start a war, but whether these orders are carried out is solely within the province of the facilitator. The facilitator might invent the consequence that the orders issued by the participants were disobeyed, or that the managers were sacked, or that there was a *coup d'état*. Such facilitator authorship need not be arbitrary. In most circumstances there could be consultation with the interested parties before the facilitator reaches a final decision.

Although facilitating is relatively enjoyable it nonetheless causes a great deal of anticipatory worry to those who have never done it before. Consequently, it is useful to look at those few occasions when things go wrong, or are totally unexpected, and see what action the facilitator could take.

To start with a mild hiccup — suppose that during the running of COMPUTER WORLD a participant turns to the facilitator and asks

'Are we allowed to meet people a second time?' or 'Are we allowed to negotiate and sign contracts?' This is to misunderstand the nature of the technique. Evidently the information that the participants are in charge of the event has been heard but not believed. The facilitator can reply 'It has nothing to do with me. I am not your boss. I am not really here.' A few replies like this will soon provoke the participants into professional behaviour. Inappropriate behaviour tends to fall into two classes:

1. taking on the role of authors of key facts;
2. taking on the role of play-actors.

In both cases perhaps the best initial response by the facilitator is to do nothing and observe whether the other participants use their role authority to sustain the event.

If someone takes on the authorship of key facts to win arguments the other participants might react by saying 'What is the evidence for that?' or 'We cannot accept unsupported statements of that nature' or 'You are telling lies'. If the authorship goes unchecked then other participants may retaliate by inventing their own facts and the event is being rapidly transformed into an ambivalent. Remedial action is best effected within the simulation itself. The facilitator can take on an appropriate temporary role (managing director, editor, messenger) and tell the participant 'There is an important telephone call for you' or some similar pretext. Having extracted the person from the action the facilitator can explain that the role is not that of a novelist and that the participant should try to get by with the facts as stated in the documents and not try to alter them to make life easier, or to 'win'. The facilitator can point out that a simulation is not a game, and that the two are incompatible.

In the second case, that of someone who starts to play-act (or play the fool), the other participants might use their role authority to call the play-actor to order by saying 'Stop play-acting' or 'If you go on like that you might find yourself looking for another job'. If this does not happen then one or two of the others might retaliate by play-acting themselves and an ambivalent has occurred. This again is not necessarily bad providing the cause is recognized. Indeed, instead of the facilitator trying to rescue the event as suggested in the paragraph above it might be worth sacrificing that particular simulation in order to provide a focus for a discussion of participant autonomy during the debriefing. The evidence would be clear — disruptive behaviour allowed to continue. The moral would be that the participants are perfectly entitled to deal with trouble makers, play-actors or any other form of aberrant action. In the real world people do clown around, tell lies, break the rules, drop out, engage in sabotage of one form or another in order to evade responsibility. In the debriefing the analysis of what went wrong can be positive and supportive both on the personal level and on group behaviour as a whole.

The two types of inappropriate behaviour discussed above are not, of course, the common or garden mistakes and misunderstandings and failures to communicate effectively which occur in almost all simulations. As in everyday life people do get it wrong, do fail to think clearly, do lack insights. What the facilitator should not do is to allow any short term anguish caused by inefficient participants to be an excuse for interfering in the action. A simulation is not a guided exercise or a rehearsed event. Success is not an essential requirement. For the facilitator to try to avoid the pain and the trauma by intervening to correct mistakes is (in almost all circumstances) to make a second and worse mistake.

Debriefing

Unlike the briefing and the action the debriefing is almost entirely dependent on the nature of the particular course and the aims of the facilitator. Since these can vary from organization to organization no firm guidelines can be laid down. At one extreme the debriefing can be appropriately lengthy while at the other extreme, as when the simulation is being used for recruitment and selection purposes only, there may be no debriefing at all.

Several general points might usefully be made. Simulations can arouse a good deal of emotion as the participants become involved in their roles and their responsibilities. What might appear at the start of the event to be a piece of paper becomes a valuable piece of property during the course of the event. A seemingly impersonal label — executive, reporter, minister — becomes a very personal thing as the event progresses. In some situations remarks can be made and participants can get hurt. All too often facilitators (even experienced ones) allow too little time for the action and when it becomes interesting allow it to overrun and curtail the debriefing. Ex-participants should always be given the time to say what they think. During the simulation some of them will almost certainly have voiced views which they do not hold in real life, or because of a deadline they might have said things they later regretted. Unless they are offered an opportunity to say their piece then dissatisfactions can go underground and may emerge later in a flurry of indignant accusations inside or outside the course itself. If the event unleashes emotions then this is a warning signal to the facilitator to treat the debriefing with understanding and circumspection.

Generally speaking it is a good idea to start by everyone taking it in turn to give a brief summary of what they did and how they felt about it, and to reveal the contents of any confidential documents.

The debriefing should not be a forum for a re-run of the arguments already voiced in the action — it should look at the implications and wider aspects, of which there are many. Here are some wider implications which readily transfer to other situations:

1. How well did each group cooperate? Did they encourage everyone to make a contribution or did someone dominate the proceedings?
2. Did individuals behave efficiently? For example, did they laboriously read through the documents starting from the beginning and working through to the end, or did they scan and select?
3. How did they handle disagreements?
4. What did they learn about themselves and their colleagues?

In most books on simulations the debriefing is regarded as a plenary session under the control of the facilitator. In keeping with the wider aims of this book the facilitator should look at other options:

- Starting the debriefing by asking the final groupings to debrief themselves and then having a plenary session.
- Changing part of the debriefing into a different format — perhaps giving participants the role of pollsters who each have a specific question and have to interview each other in pairs.
- Moving the event into a follow-on simulation based on what might happen next — a meeting of the board of directors, a public inquiry, an action for libel.
- Having a short 'Get it off your chests' debriefing followed by a later debriefing to allow participants time to collect evidence, write reports, obtain interviews, and have second thoughts about what happened and why.
- Asking different groups to concentrate on specific aspects — company efficiency, communications, group dynamics, authority, the media, publicity, innovation, personnel problems — and to report their findings.
- Changing the format of the debriefings after one or two simulations in order to provide new opportunities, insights, and challenges.

One final point can be made concerning debriefings which involves a potentially sensitive area — the existing hierarchy of the organization. In some simulations a person who has a top position in real life, whether in the boardroom or in a street gang, can behave uncharacteristically in a simulation in order to preserve their dignity and real life status. Should the facilitator refer to such episodes in the debriefing? If not, then what should the facilitator do if other people mention the episode — give a dismissive shrug, make a bland remark, or point out that such behaviour is interesting and invite discussion?

As with most personality issues there is no general answer to problems of hierarchy except to say that the wisest course for the facilitator is to think about the question before it arises, and if it does arise then appraise the situation correctly, take into account all the circumstances, and behave appropriately.

Chapter 3

The style of the ten simulations

Simplicity of format, subtlety of action

A broad distinction can be made between simulations which aim to reproduce various functions of the workplace for specific job training and simulations which aim for the transfer of general skills. The first type might be called specific and the second transferable. Note that these two labels are attached to aims only, not to the materials or what actually happens.

Specific simulations
The usual aim is to provide a hands-on experience of certain routines which are part of the job. For airline pilots the equipment can include a flight simulator of a particular aircraft, for counter clerks or sales staff it can be a simulated workplace encounter with customers, for clerical staff it can involve the company's office routines, for business executives it can involve decision making related to the policy of the company. It is a common mistake to suppose that the designers of such simulations try to simulate the whole of the working environment. What happens in practice is that the author is selective and picks out those features which are deemed important or those elements which can be best learned in isolation from other elements. The scenario can be tailored to highlight the usual or the unusual, the easy or the difficult, the simple or the complicated, the trivial or the potentially disastrous. Although the author is likely to aim to keep the scenario relatively simple wherever possible, the nature of the job may entail background and instructional documents which are very bulky — office instructions, flight manuals, computer codes and procedures. A common secondary aim is to learn facts about the organization, which means that the 'facts' of the event must be real (or at least typical of that organization) and not fictitious.

Transference simulations
The usual aim is to provide opportunities for the maximum amount of participant interaction with the minimum amount of pre-packaged information — unless, of course, the aim is to give experience in dealing

with a mass of data. Transference simulations usually have a simple format. Often the scenario is fictitious since this is a more efficient way of producing balanced arguments, interest, interaction than would be the case if the author was constrained by solid immovable facts.

Although in theory these two types are not mutually exclusive, in practice there are usually clear differences. Specific simulations tend to be routine, practical, repetitive, with the participants knowing that their job is to learn the skills and facts. The authors are often the training personnel themselves. The simulations sometimes have too many facts for their own good, and can lack the elegance in design usually associated with published simulations. Transferable simulations are often published simulations, if only because the cost of organizations producing their own would almost certainly be greater in time and salaries than buying them ready-made. With published simulations there is some assurance that they really do work.

Despite these differences the two types are not rivals since they are aiming at different objectives. Neither is a substitute for the other. It is not possible to say 'This type is best' without considering the context.

Since the above categorization is based on aims, not materials or what actually happens, it is inevitable that aims are not always achieved and that boundary lines are fudged. Computerized business management simulations are a case in point. A question rarely asked is whether the label 'management' is justified. It is usually assumed from the label that it is a simulation in the transferable skills category. Looking behind the labels at what happens in practice often reveals highly repetitive rounds of number crunching. In the first round the participants might be thinking 'We are managers of a chocolate factory' but by the time the third or fourth round comes along they have forgotten about the chocolate and are thinking 'How can we crack the code in the computer'. Such simulations have more to do with mathematical puzzles rather than the day-to-day activities of business management. Missing are people — trade unions, strikes, personnel problems, law, values, the environment. If any of these real world events are introduced into the computer simulation they are usually random numbers in disguise, and are no more part of management than a 'Go to jail' instruction in Monopoly. Because such simulations are usually costly in time and money this tends to give the impression that they are also cost effective in developing managerial skills. There have been glaring examples in which the investment cost of computerized simulations has meant that trainers have continued to run them year after year because no one has had the courage (or the authority) to point out that they were not achieving the intended results.

All the simulations in this book deal with management issues as distinct from mathematical problems. Even OUTERWORLD

The style of the ten simulations

TRADE, which has several rounds of development and trading, involves negotiation between countries plus broadcasts, and is about people as well as production.

One of the main criteria in the design of the ten simulations is the encouragement of a high level of interaction. There are no passive or part-time roles. There are no gender roles which might impede interaction and possibly cause embarrassment. Instead, the roles are functional to give maximum opportunities for decision making with professional intent. No personality transplants are required. People remain themselves and have to do the best they can in the situations in which they find themselves. The simulations aim for plausibility and consistency in interesting situations. Although basically simple in design, considerable subtlety (even deviousness) often emerges from the participants themselves when they realize the opportunities for managerial initiatives.

Varied, unusual, open ended

The variety and diversity of these simulations is partly to encourage open thinking and open learning. All too often management courses are based on repetitions of particular types of decision making, and this can leave people unprepared and unable to cope when something unusual crops up. The varied simulations in this book allow participants to gain experience in dealing with the unexpected, which is a valuable aspect of good management.

Another consideration is that the interaction is transferable not only to job functions but also to human beings on a personal level. For example, the skill of diplomats, the news sense of journalists, the personnel considerations of management, the subtlety of secret agents are useful experiences, not only in the area of management but also in the home, or at the club.

All the simulations are open ended so as to encourage flexibility and initiatives as distinct from the 'What does the instruction book say?' mentality. Asking a good question can be at least as important as providing a good answer. In designing these simulations the key facts are used to balance arguments – unlike some simulations which attempt to manipulate people in favour of 'good' causes and 'right' outcomes. One consequence of non-manipulation is that it makes it less easy for people to take shelter and claim 'We thought you wanted us to do it that way and to decide such-and-such'. Thus, they are provoked and impelled by the lack of instruction into thinking for themselves and taking professional responsibility for what they do.

It must be admitted that not all participants find this to their liking. For those who prefer subservience (or laziness) the cry 'We don't know what we are supposed to do' sometimes means 'We can't be bothered to think for ourselves, so why don't you just tell us how to find the right answer?' Such attitudes are not restricted to teenagers. However, the information in the Notes for Participants and the overall design of the ten simulations should reduce or prevent such attitudes.

Many simulations attempt to achieve participant involvement by emphasizing competition, scoring, winning. Thus, they tend to become ambivalents with some people trying to win while other are behaving with real world considerations in mind. In some of the simulations in this book there is competition, but the balance of emphasis is on cooperation, sympathy, understanding, help. There are no conflict-orientated personality stereotypes. No role card says 'You do not like X's attitude'. There are no roles for 'Joe Bloggs the abrasive reporter' or 'Sally Bloggs the shy citizen'. Unlike some simulations there are no roles for the vulnerable, for children, for the relatives of people suffering from terminal diseases, or for people being evicted from their homes by rapacious landlords.

Not only are the roles functional and neutral, there are no roles which specify gender or race or age. There is nothing on the lines of 'Imagine that you are a 12-year-old girl', or 'You are a black person who has suffered from harassment'. This means that anyone can take part without being made to feel uncomfortable by being asked to adopt another personality, another age, or sex, or culture.

Participant roles involving managing the event's mechanics
Some of these simulations involve participants organizing part of the event, not as facilitators from outside the simulations, but as organizers within them. In STOP TALKING the executives have the job of organising an event for trainers. In PEG SPOTTING the assessors at the Ministry of Careers have to organize and assess tests. In LINK MANAGEMENT the hotel managers have to organize a simulation in which companies compete for the contract of providing entertainments for children.

This Russian doll aspect is quite deliberate. The interlocking events, the simulations within simulations, organizations within organizations, is to give practice in management of people as distinct from making decisions about where to site an oil drilling platform. Thus, one avenue in the debriefings is to explore what the managers thought of the people they managed, and vice versa.

It is not difficult to extend the application of this hands-on management experience to allowing the trainees and students to run the simulations themselves. Individuals or groups could take it in turns to be facilitator, and this could have a desirable influence on the course as a whole, increasing consultation and cooperation between staff and trainees. This could provide the organizing teams with a sense of ownership and achievement which is a natural extension of the participant power within the simulations themselves. There are some indications that facilitators are becoming more inclined to ask the participants to run the events, perhaps because of increasing familiarity with the technique. It is an option which helps to avoid the situation in which the staff are firmly in control of events and the students think of themselves as trainee fodder.

Built-in follow-up opportunities

The ten simulations generate experiences and ideas which lend themselves to follow-up activities. An example was mentioned earlier — in STOP TALKING the participants might produce outlines of exercises and simulations which could be developed and become part of the course.

The most obvious area for follow-up is the subject or skill area of the simulation — the media, advertising, bargaining, assessing.

Interest in media presentation could result in a run of OUTERWORLD TRADE, PAPER LAUNCH, COMPUTER WORLD and ROCK ISLAND. If the area was the assessment of personnel then relevant simulations would be STOP TALKING, PAPER LAUNCH, PEG SPOTTING, FORT, and LINK MANAGEMENT. If negotiation is the issue then this could motivate the choice of CAN WE SAVE LOGO MOTORS?, OUTERWORLD TRADE, COMPUTER WORLD, SELLING THE FLAG. If 'design and build' is the follow-up theme then there are the experiences in STOP TALKING, PAPER LAUNCH, PEG SPOTTING, FORT, and LINK MANAGEMENT.

These experiences can be used for future learning not merely in the debriefings or follow-up but almost any time. It could be in the form of spontaneous remarks — 'Just like the Trumpet advert', or 'That's the EconAdvice memo all over again'.

In all ten simulations various events will occur and various remarks will be made which will be worthy of pursuit. It is really a matter of the facilitator listening and observing and drawing conclusions. This is not too difficult since the facilitator is in an ideal position to observe. With practice it becomes relatively easy to pick cherries out of the cake, since after running the simulations a few times the unusual remarks and ideas stand out like red fruit.

Another follow-up avenue occurs if the participants are allowed to run the simulations. Not only does the learning and enjoyment index rise appreciably but there is usually a keener demand to follow up various points. If the participants organize the debriefing then they too will be concerned with follow-up ideas which may well help to integrate the simulations with the course, and vice versa. Feedback on the value of the course will become more obvious through the spread of ownership. It removes a good deal of anxiety that is reflected in end-of-course questionnaires asking 'What did you think of the course and what improvements do you suggest?' It could even make the questionnaires redundant.

A different type of follow-up occurs when simulations are run for recruitment and selection purposes. Here the follow-up may not be in the form of a traditional debriefing but in personal interviews about a person's career.

There is nothing new in the idea of simulations for selecting personnel. The first institutional use of simulations is usually attributed to the Prussian Army in the nineteenth century and arose through dissatisfaction with the recruitment of officers based on interviews and pencil and paper tests. Various simulations were set up which tested those qualities which are desirable in officers — leadership, obedience, etc. The technique was later developed by the British Army. During the Second World War an American Army officer who had been in Britain studying army selection procedures imported the simulation idea into the United States for the training of spies. Earlier attempts to recruit the criminal classes for 'dirty' work had resulted in several disastrous operations in the field. Selection courses were devised which consisted of virtually nothing else but simulations. A development from these experiences was that the Americans saw that the principle for selecting spies and officers applied equally to the selection of managers — simply looking at the job and then finding the simulations which gave opportunities for the qualities required. Thus began Assessment Centres (see OSS 1948, Moses 1977 and others) which use simulations as a regular feature of recruitment and selection. (The word 'Centre' is used to cover any place where the selection procedures are held.) The research literature indicates that assessment centres are a good deal more effective and reliable than interview and pencil and paper assessments, which is really stating the obvious if interpersonal behaviour is an important quality in the job.

To sum up, although any of the ten simulations could be run as a one-off event there are considerable advantages in using several or all of the ten. They become easier with practice, the developmental aspect becomes important, the lessons learned in one simulation can be put into practice in the next, the follow-up becomes more professional. Thus, the use of simulations within the course can be deliberately planned to increase the managerial efficiency of the course as a whole.

Part Two
The Ten Simulations

Simulation	Minimum number of participants	Minimum hours required
1. STOP TALKING	8	2
2. PAPER LAUNCH	6	1
3. CAN WE SAVE LOGO MOTORS?	8	2
4. OUTERWORLD TRADE	12	2
5. PEG SPOTTING	12	1 ½
6. FORT	6	1
7. LINK MANAGEMENT	10	1 ½
8. COMPUTER WORLD	8	1 ½
9. ROCK ISLAND	6	1 ½
10. SELLING THE FLAG	10	1 ½

Order

The simulations can be run in any order appropriate to the course. (See suggestions on pages 26-8.)

Numbers

There is no maximum number of participants. It depends on the size of the room(s). With large numbers there is the option of running two or more identical events simultaneously.

Time

The minimum times include briefing and debriefing. When running any of the simulations for the first time it is advisable to add half an hour to the minimum time and see how it goes. All ten simulations can be adjourned at almost any point to fit into more than one session.

Technology

If information technology is used this will probably increase the amount of time required, particularly if the participants are expected to aim for semi-professional standards.

46   The ten simulations

STOP TALKING

Facilitator's notes

Skills: technique awareness, authorship, cooperation, assessing, planning.
Note: In management courses this is a useful simulation to begin with — see page 27. In non-management courses note the option of starting with PAPER LAUNCH – see pages 27–8.
Time: 2-3 hours, including briefing and debriefing.
Numbers: The minimum number is 8 (2 senior executives and 6 trainers). With larger numbers arrange for about one participant out of 4 or 5 to be a senior executive. The maximum number is limited only by the size of the room(s).
Photocopying: One copy of Notes for Participants and the *Aze News* for each participant. One copy of Consultancy Document — Appendix C for each executive.
Materials and facilities. Scrap paper is essential. Two rooms are useful, but if only one is available then the trainers and executives should be separated by as much distance as possible. If coffee can be provided then this will increase realism.
Briefing: Set a time for the executives to arrive at the Staff Training Department (STD), preferably not more than 10 minutes into the action (15 minutes with school children), so that the trainers can get to work devising the materials as quickly as possible.
Action: Straightforward. If the simulation takes place in one room then it is a good idea to ask the executives to move out into the corridor for a minute or two before arriving at STD.
Debriefing: One aspect can be a joint assessment of the outlines. The simulation outlines should include the following four points (in any order):
1. The problem? (personnel matters, sales, fashions, plans)
2. The roles? (sales staff, designers, managers, customers, rivals)
3. What to do? (discuss, design, write reports, make decisions)
4. What with? (sales figures, clothing, media, existing knowledge)
Outlines for the exercises should include points 1, 3 and 4, but not point 2. Do not mention the four points in the briefing, let the participants try to work it out for themselves from the documents.

Other questions for the debriefing: Did the trainers welcome the executives when they arrived? How well did the executives explain the situation? Did the trainers subdivide into groups to produce more outlines? Did the executives use the event as part of the assessment procedures for a new head of STD? Could any of the outlines be adapted and developed to fit the course? Were simulations and exercises distinguished from games and role-play (see pages 13-16)?

STOP TALKING

Notes for participants

Roles
1. Senior executives of Aze Clothing Group
2. Trainers in Aze Clothing Group

Documents
1. Extracts from *Aze News*
2. Consultancy Document — Appendix C (for senior executives only)

Situation
It is the day of the publication of the house magazine *Aze News*. Senior executives of the Aze Clothing Group are to visit the Group's Staff Training Department (STD). They will be bringing with them part of a consultancy document which recommends improvements in STD's methods which in the past have been based on instructional methods, not on group activities. The whole of the day at STD has been cleared of training schedules and the senior executives are due to arrive shortly before the morning coffee break.

Events
The simulation begins with senior executives meeting on the eighth floor of Head Office while the trainers meet at STD. The second stage is what happens when the senior executives arrive at STD.

Conditions
You must behave with professional intent, which includes bearing in mind what you hope for in your career in the Aze Clothing Group.

You must not invent 'facts' to win arguments but you can invent details if they are plausible and consistent with the facts in the documents.

You can do anything you have not been told not to do, but you must accept your roles and your responsibilities.

Aze News

OUR 'YOUTH IMAGE'

The *Annual Report* published last week says that the Aze Clothing Group has a competitive edge and that the 'youth image' is paying off despite increasing competition in the retail clothing trade. There were profits of 23.6 million (after tax), roughly the same as last year, and dividends were maintained. Eight new high street shops were opened, three were closed, and the loss-making Razan Shoe Company was sold. The Group's position as one of the leading clothing and fashion houses has been strengthened by providing joint finance for pop videos with accompanying advertising. Future plans include the manufacture of sports equipment and the production of some educational materials, as yet unspecified, for schools and colleges.

CONSULTANCY COMPLETED

The outside management consultants who have been investigating the operating position of the Aze Clothing Group have completed their work and their recommendations have been approved by the Board of Directors. Meetings will take place between senior executives and Heads of Departments to discuss any action required. The first meeting takes place today at STD and will look at the possibility of including simulations and exercises in the training courses.

GOODBYE E.R.

A special party to mark the retirement of E.R. George was held in STD last week. E.R., who has been Head of Staff Training for the last 15 years decided to take early retirement and will be much missed. E.R. will be remembered by many of today's staff for giving clear and effective lectures about the Aze Clothing Group and its policies. It was E.R. who broke new ground in the late 1970s by producing a training package of videos showing the shops, clothes, customers, advertising, and the backroom people — secretaries, planners, buyers, canteen staff, and there were shots of E.R. describing how to deal with difficult customers.

SUGGESTIONS BOX

At art school we had an exercise to design a fashion theme for the winter. Later this was made into a simulation in which we had to do the same thing but everyone had a role — designers, buyers, advertisers, customers. Why can't STD have this sort of thing?
R. Vincenti (Sales Dept)

CONSULTANCY DOCUMENT — APPENDIX C

Staff Training Department

Findings For training purposes STD relies on direct instructional methods. The trainers are excellent in conveying information about the design, manufacture and sale of clothes.

Conclusions The trainers talk too much. The training packages contain no simulations or exercises. The trainers have little evidence of how well the trainees can work in teams, or of their ability in any situations other than interviews and lectures. The trainers are not in a position to identify management potential.

Proposals We propose that senior executives should visit STD and organize and run the following activities:

1. Explain to the trainers that in view of the lack of simulations and exercises the aim of the session is to create, in outline only, as many simulations and exercises as possible in the time available.
2. Divide the trainers at random into two groups. Ask one group to create outlines of simulations and ask the other group to create outlines of exercises.
3. Explain that all simulations have roles (customers, sales staff, clothes designers, rival company, etc) whereas exercises have no roles and the trainees remain as trainees. All simulations and exercises must have a problem for the participants to tackle rather than just facts to be learned.
4. Tell the trainers to produce outlines which mention the sort of documents which would be used and, if it is a simulation, specify the roles. Emphasize that outlines only are required. The trainers should avoid writing any of the documents or role cards which would be used within the events.
5. Set a time limit.
6. During the action do not answer such questions as 'Do you think this is a good idea?' Tell them that you are observers and that if they have any questions they should ask each other.
7. After the time has expired, discuss the outcome with the trainers.

Results From the point of view of the executives the activity is likely to reveal more than just the outlines of simulations and exercises.

50 The ten simulations

PAPER LAUNCH

Facilitator's notes

Skills: market planning, authorship, publicity, presentation.

Time: 1-2 hours, but if desktop publishing and video cameras and editing facilities are used and if the participants aim for semi-professional standards then the event could last for several days.

Numbers: Three groups of between 2 and 6 in a group. With about 20 participants there can be a fourth or fifth group representing the TV authority or the Advertising Standards Committee. With 20–40 participants run it as two separate events.

Photocopying: One copy of Notes for Participants and of *Media Matters* for each participant.

Materials and facilities: Scrap paper essential. Art facilities — large sheets of paper, coloured pens — should be provided. Other possibilities include musical instruments (for jingles), tape recorders, etc, perhaps discussed in advance with the participants. Video equipment should be used only if the operators are skilled. Some sort of 'studio', if only a table and a couple of chairs, needs to be organized for the broadcasts (see pages 29–30). It helps the broadcasters if a clock with a second hand is available.

Briefing: Discuss the timing of the advertisements and also in which order they should be given. Outline the facilities available. It helps to create a professional sense of urgency if the broadcast times are firm deadlines — perhaps 'Because the studio technicians refuse to work overtime and if the broadcasters are not ready on time then the advertisement is not transmitted'.

Action: Routine.

Debriefing: If media presentation is an important feature of the course then a subsequent (or delayed) debriefing session is valuable because it allows people time to look closely at the actual words and images used in the advertisements rather than judging them by immediate impressions only. If real life media experts were invited to the simulation then this would provide a more professional appraisal of the advertisements during the debriefing. There are plenty of opportunities for follow-up activities including research, critical viewing of advertisements, and other media events.

PAPER LAUNCH

Notes for participants

Roles
Advertisers and newspaper executives in the Republic of Logo.

Document
Extract from *Media Matters*, the trade magazine of the Logon media.

Situation
For the past ten years the two main newspapers have been the tabloid *Bugle* and the quality paper *Flute*. A new paper called the *Tambourine* is being launched to try to capture the middle ground. In retaliation both the *Bugle* and *Flute* are to produce bumper issues and a special colour magazine on *Tambourine's* launch day. The three newspapers have each bought time for a 2 minute television commercial on the eve of launch day.

Event
Three publicity teams each design and transmit a 2 minute television commercial for their newspapers.

Conditions
You must behave with professional intent, which includes bearing in mind what might happen to your own career and the future of your newspaper and/or advertising business.

You must not invent 'facts' to win arguments or to enhance your own position, but you can invent peripheral details provided they are plausible and consistent with the facts in the materials.

You can do anything you have not been told not to do.

Media Matters

CHASING THE PAPER READERS

Both sides in the long-standing *Bugle–Flute* battle for readers are now directing their fire at a new rival, the *Tambourine*, which is being launched next week.

Over the past ten years the combined sales figure of the *Bugle* and *Flute* has risen by 5 million — from 25 to 30 million copies a year. Last year saw the up-market *Flute* take a million readers away from the down-market *Bugle*.

Current sales figures (in millions) related to economic classes of readers — A (high), B (middle) and C (low) — show that the expanding and influential middle class is a prime target for all three papers.

Tambourine management believes that the middle class in Logo, mainly class B, is badly served by both existing papers and that not only is class B up for grabs but there is also a potential for class B buying more papers.

The reason why *Flute* has done relatively well this year at the expense of the tabloid is probably because it increased its coverage of sport. The *Tambourine* will also aim at good sports pages and may decide to concentrate on areas where the other two papers are vulnerable, such as fashions, the home and (possibly) educational matters. However, the *Bugle* and *Flute* are hitting back on launch day by each producing a special colour supplement and will continue to promote their Saturday colour supplements. The *Tambourine* does not have the capacity to produce colour supplements at present, but may acquire the facility depending on the first few months of sales.

All three papers have purchased 2 minute TV advertising slots for the eve of launch day. A silent watcher of these L-day presentations will be the Government's Advertising Standards Committee. Exaggerated claims, unfair knocking of the competition, or deliberate misrepresentations are likely to receive rather more than just a gentle tut-tut response from the watchdogs. Serious falls from standards would certainly result in heavy fines.

Paper	Total	Class A	Class B	Class C
Bugle	20	1	6	13
Flute	10	3	5	2
	30	4	11	15

54   *The ten simulations*

CAN WE SAVE LOGO MOTORS?

Facilitator's notes

Skills: analysing, planning, negotiating, decision making.
Time: 2–3 hours, including briefing and debriefing.
Numbers: Between 8 and 24 participants. With 8 there would be four groups of 2 in the first stage, and two groups of 4 in the second stage. If the total number is not divisible by four then during the second stage there can be two participants in one role at some of the top level meetings. With more than 24 the participants can be divided into two, and two events can then run in parallel.
Photocopying: One copy of Notes for Participants for each participant. Four copies each of the Selected Library List and all six library documents. One copy only of each of the five memos.
Materials and facilities: Scrap paper, ruled paper for documents. If only one room is available the teams should be as far apart as possible. There should be space (facilitator's table perhaps) for the library. As each group may need copies of their own draft documents to take to top level meetings it is desirable (but not essential) that photocopiers, word processors, typewriters (or even carbon paper) be made available. Other realistic touches might include coffee, carafes of water, boardroom paraphernalia.
Briefing: Discuss furniture arrangements for stages 1 and 2. Decide whether there should be a full supply or library documents (i.e. one for each team) or whether there should be fewer copies with time limits on borrowing, and reservation forms? Both parts of the simulation should have a firm deadline in order to avoid one group hanging around waiting for the others to finish, but deadlines could be re-negotiated according to developments. It is advisable to allow about one third of the total time for stage one and two thirds for the meetings of the Committee of Four, which can always adjourn from time to time to take another look at the documents.
Action: Straightforward. It may be preferable to give the EconAdvice team only their first memo when the action starts; delaying handing out the reply memo for 5 minutes will increase its impact.
Debriefing: As this simulation is probably the closest to the traditional idea of management simulations the debriefing can follow the usual lines — a plenary session with the facilitator in charge looking at (a) what happened, (b) whether the participants behaved efficiently, imaginatively, appropriately, and (c) comparing the outcome with examples from the real world of lame duck industries. Another option is to start by keeping the groups in their final positions and letting them debrief themselves and then have a joint debriefing. For other options see pages 34–6.

CAN WE SAVE LOGO MOTORS?

Notes for participants

Roles
First stage roles: middle management of four organizations — Logo Motors, the independent consultancy firm EconAdvice, the Automobile Workers' Union, and the Ministry of Economic Development.
Second stage roles: bosses of these four organizations.

Documents
1. Confidential memos for each of the four groups.
2. Six documents in the library, plus the list of these six items.

Situation
Logo Motors, one of the largest companies in the Republic of Logo, makes cars at its main factory at Rackley and produces motor bikes and mopeds at its factory at Turl. The company is in serious financial trouble. The Government has set up a 'Committee of Four' to see if Logo Motors can be saved. (The Logon unit of currency is the Lo, pronounced 'low'.)

Events
In the first part, middle management executives meet separately in their own four groups to discuss the situation. In the second part, each participant takes on the role of boss within their organization, and the four groups split up with participants going to different top-level meetings which take place simultaneously.

Conditions
You must behave with professional intent, which includes bearing in mind what you hope for in your career.

You must not invent 'facts' to win arguments, but you can invent details if they are plausible and consistent with the facts in the documents.

You can do anything you have not been told not to do, but you must accept your roles and responsibilities.

Logo Motors

MEMORANDUM

From: Managing Director, LM
To: Executive Advisory Committee, LM

Before I sit down at the Committee of Four I want a clear picture of the following:

1. Logo Motors' present situation
2. The available options for the future

What I want is a summary of points, all on one page, setting out the whole thing neatly and precisely. Give me something I can hand round to the others. Take a look at the report of our motor bikes and mopeds in Compare.

> Re Sunday Sentinel's article: I have had a word with the head of our Research and Development Department who tells me that the designs for the Sabrina do exist, and that it would take about 3 years to develop. The cost of a small amount of re-designing, plus building and testing the prototypes, would be about 200 million Lo for the 3 years.

In addition to providing the one page summary I want your confidential recommendations on a separate sheet of paper. What do we hope for, what should we press for, what would we be willing to accept?

Naturally you should consider what should be done about repaying the 100 million government loan and whether we could do anything to attract further Government assistance.

I need hardly say that your recommendations should be positive: I do not intend to be the captain of a sinking ship.

Automobile Workers' Union

MEMO

From: General Secretary AWU
To: Research Committee (LM)

Take a look at today's Logon Gazette. You will see the rumour, which may or may not be true, that the Government might be secretly pleased if Logo Motors went out of business. Taking account of the facts, as distinct from the gossip, I want you to give me:

1. The options
2. The advantages
3. The disadvantages
4. Your recommendations

I want the whole thing on one page, no more. I want a neat summary of the situation as seen from the point of view of the auto workers. I don't want an essay or a chunk from an article. I may hand your document to the others on the committee.

If you want to make any confidential recommendations on a separate sheet of paper for my eyes only then please do so. If Logo Motors went out of business then our next annual conference would be a gathering of the unemployed.

Ministry of Economic Development

MEMORANDUM

From: Minister, E.Dev.
To: Research Committee. LM situ.

Please effect with immediate priority the following:

1. Summarise up-date position of Logo Motors
2. List options open to LM and Government

Please comply with the above in a single page covering everything that is relevant. Note – I may wish to put your document on the table at the meeting as a starting point for discussion.

Two points should be ignored in your summary:

(a) The trade union call (see Gazette) for import restrictions on cars. Such action would almost certainly provoke retaliation by other countries against our exports, including LM cars and motor bikes. Also, the general trend of Government policy is to reduce and not increase barriers to international trade.

(b) Ignore the rumour (also Gazette) that the Government would be happy to see Logo Motors go out of business. The Government's position is unchanged from that stated by the Prime Minister in Parliament last month – 'The Government wishes to see Logo Motors established as a viable enterprise and not a burden to the taxpayer.'

In addition to the summary of the position please provide me with your confidential recommendations written on a separate sheet of paper, including what action might be desirable and/or acceptable to the Ministry, particularly in relation to the 100 million government loan to Logo Motors which is still outstanding.

EconAdvice

Memorandum (LM/1 23rd Nov)

From: LM Account team
To: Executive Director

At the end of our 4 week investigation we have devised an effective plan which would save Logo Motors.

1. The abandonment of the Ahmed car, entailing 2,500 redundancies at the Rackley factory, about half the work-force there.
2. Development of the Sabrina car. (See Sunday Sentinel)
3. The Government should (for once) be generous and write off the debt of 100 million Lo.

The following table compares last year's figures with the estimated figures under the above plan (in millions of Lo):

Car production		Last year	Estimated
Costs: materials		376	190
wages		108	70
overheads		132	100
redundancy payments			20
total costs		616	380
Sales: (Ahmed	45)		
(Olaf	384)	429	(Olaf) 380
Loss		187	nil

With the Rackley factory streamlining on producing the Olaf, the development of the Sabrina could occupy space on the same site and would cost somewhere between 100 and 300 million Lo in research and development costs spread over a 3 year period. This could be covered by profits from the motorbike/moped production at Turl.

The fiercest opposition to the plan is likely to come from the Automobile Workers Union, so the 20 million in redundancy money is about 50% higher than the minimum required by industrial law. The estimated wage bill of 70 million takes into account a wage rise of roughly 15% compared with the current inflation rate of 10%, but this could be attached to a so-called productivity deal so that the Government can justify the expenditure to the taxpayers. This leaves last year's loss of 187 million. Most of this could be paid off by the sale at reduced prices of the large stocks of unsold Ahmed cars, and the sale of some showroom space.

The ten simulations

EconAdvice

Memorandum (LM/2. 24th Nov)

From: Executive Director
To: LM Account team

Your memo is unacceptable. I want something that I can show to the others at the Committee of Four, not a plan wrapped up in funny remarks and insults.

Do the following:

1. Extract from the memorandum the table of figures on production costs and sales. I can circulate this at a suitable opportunity at the top level meeting.

2. Produce a second sheet which I can circulate if required giving further details of your plan. Keep it short and crisp.

   (a) Do not recommend the plan. I can do that at the meeting.

   (b) Don't add glory words, e.g 'effective'.

   (c) Omit clumsy and ungrammatical jargon - for example 'Rackley factory streamlining on producing the Olaf'.

   (d) Don't add insulting references about lack of Government generosity, 'so-called productivity deal', etc. Do not say such things as 'See Sunday Sentinel'. They are professionals and will have looked up the references before coming to the meeting; if not then I shall have the pleasure of enlightening them.

```
Selected Library List
```

*Logo Motors and related items - as requested

Journal/Newspaper	Title of item	Publication date
Logon Gazette	Government Acts to Save LM	today
Official Statistics	Sales: cars, motorbikes/mopeds	yesterday
Company Comments	Logo Motors - a bleak future?	last week
Money Monthly	Inflation and unemployment	last week
Sunday Sentinel	Sabrina - the car that never was	last month
Compare	Two-wheel transport (powered)	last month

Logon Gazette

GOVERNMENT ACTS TO SAVE LM

by our industrial correspondent

The Government has intervened in the financial crisis at Logo Motors by appointing a top-level committee to investigate the affairs of the Company and make recommendations.

Perhaps as a last hope for the ailing LM giant the Minister of Economic Development is to chair a Committee of Four, the other three being the Managing Director of Logo Motors, the leader of the Automobile Workers' Union and the Executive Director of the independent consultancy firm EconAdvice which has been trying to find a way to rescue LM. EconAdvice is believed to have come up with a plan.

Worried by LM's drift into massive debt and by the large numbers of unsold Ahmed cars, the Government has decided to force a decision one way or another. According to an unofficial source it may be prepared to face short term unpopularity and let Logo Motors go out of business altogether. Although the manufacture of motor bikes and mopeds at LM's Turl factory makes a profit, the car factory at Rackley is losing huge sums of money daily.

A trade union rally in Logo City yesterday called on the Government to impose tough restrictions on imports of foreign cars.

CAN WE SAVE LOGO MOTORS? 63

Compare

TWO-WHEEL TRANSPORT (POWERED)

Powered two-wheel transport is increasing in popularity in Logo and throughout the region. The reasons include the increased popularity of motor bikes in sporting activities and also the need of business and commerce for such vehicles — for example to deliver urgent parcels.

The Logon market is dominated by the Logo Motors division at Turl which manufactures the Midas range of mopeds and the Minerva range of motor bikes. Together these account for some 75% of sales. The remaining 25% are foreign imports, mainly the Speedong range of mopeds and the Zip range of motor bikes.

In order to compare the value and quality of these vehicles we chose two pairs of products, each pair being roughly the same price and engine capacity. We used four measures of comparison — reliability, comfort, handling, and running costs, and these were assessed on a 5-point scale ranging from poor (1) to good (5). As well as our own testing we sent a questionnaire to our members and received nearly 200 replies. Using both the questionnaire replies and the testing we have compiled the following table:

Type	Name	Reliability	Comfort	Handling	Running costs
Moped	Midas	4	4	4	4
Moped	Speedong	2	3	5	3
Motor bike	Minerva	4	4	3	4
Motor bike	Zip	3	3	4	3

We conclude that all four machines are average or above, apart from some doubt about the reliability of the Speedong. Those who filled in our questionnaire clearly preferred the Logo Motors machines, the Midas and the Minerva.

Best buys: Midas moped. Minerva motor bike.

Official Statistics

Sales of cars, motor bikes, mopeds

Category	last year	2 years ago	3 years ago	4 years ago
Logo Motors cars — home sales				
Ahmed (large)	1 228	3 407	6 889	–
Olaf (medium)	15 561	17 996	18 541	20 223
Logo Motors cars — export sales				
Ahmed (large)	210	1 076	2 104	–
Olaf (medium)	3 421	3 581	3 966	4 757
Foreign cars — imports				
Kodiak (large)	3 555	4 103	5 681	8 510
Tiger (medium)	11 419	14 296	17 947	21 109
Gerbil (small)	27 605	26 920	26 541	26 111
Logo Motors 2-wheeled — home sales				
Minerva range (motor bikes)	32 987	32 110	27 002	25 089
Midas range (mopeds)	40 004	35 971	29 552	28 983
Logo Motors 2-wheeled — exports				
Minerva range (motor bikes)	26 323	25 055	22 080	21 876
Midas range (mopeds)	44 982	36 734	30 734	29 111
Foreign 2-wheeled — imports				
Zip range (motorbikes)	11 103	8 117	7 709	7 195
Speedong range (mopeds)	10 426	9 992	8 599	7 003

Company Comments

Logo Motors — a bleak future?

The annual report and accounts of Logo motors reveals a position even worse than had been revealed earlier. Last year's accounts, which showed a profit of only 21 million Lo has been followed this year by losses of 118 million. Whereas last year's report spoke of 'a reasonable hope of extra sales' this year's report refers to 'unavoidable losses caused by the generally depressed state of the economy and sharper foreign competition'.

Three years ago LM borrowed 100 million Lo from the government and repayment is due in six months time; it is difficult to see how this can be done. The Turl plant (Minerva motor bikes and Midas mopeds) continues to be successful, but the Rackley plant (Ahmed and Olaf cars) is now running at a loss of over 180 million. There were some technical faults (now rectified) in the Ahmed, not to mention frequent industrial disputes at Rackley. Anyone passing the Rackley factory will have noticed the depressingly large number of unsold cars lined up like last year's diaries.

The decline in LM's fortunes can be seen in comparing the profits over the last four years.

	Profits (in millions)			
	last year	2 years ago	3 years ago	4 years ago
Cars	−187	−38	45	101
Motor bikes/mopeds	69	59	54	48
Total	−118	21	99	149

An analysis of the loss of 187 million at Rackley reveals the following:

Costs (in millions)

Materials (including components)	376
Wages	108
Overheads, advertising, etc.	132
	616

Sales Ahmed 45
Olaf 384   429
Loss   187

Conclusion — a bleak outlook for management and workers alike.

Sunday Sentinel

SABRINA — THE CAR THAT NEVER WAS

.... by the Sunday Sentinel Investigation Team

Eight years ago, at the July meeting of the Board of Management of Logo Motors, ten executives spent 3 hours 50 minutes examining the design of two cars — the large Ahmed and the compact Sabrina. Only one could be produced. Which one? A vote was taken and the meeting split 5–5. The casting vote was with the (then) Managing Director, Leon Nardini. 'We need prestige' declared Nardini. 'We'll go big. We'll go for the Ahmed.' It was the wrong decision taken at the wrong time by the wrong man.

Nardini, a man of considerable ambition and talent, had a failing. He wanted glory. What happened is well known. The Ahmed sales slumped from 9,000 a year to 1,400 in three years. Technical faults and high fuel consumption deterred customers. Two years ago Nardini resigned, taking up an advisory post abroad with a petro-chemical company.

But what happened to the Sabrina? Our investigation team have discovered that not only did Nardini choose the Ahmed, he also imposed a ban on any mention of the Sabrina. The car, the drawings, and even the name was marked 'confidential'. Our team understands that the design still exists in the files of LM's Research and Development Department — a department savagely cut in an economy drive during the past year. Whether the drawings could still be used as the basis for a small car, production is doubtful, but might be worth exploring. Otherwise the failure of Logo Motors, at least at the Rackley factory, is in jeopardy and 5,000 jobs at Rackley are at stake plus another few thousand jobs in firms making components for the Ahmed and Olaf. To launch a new car — which would not be in the showrooms for another three years — would be a risky business. But Logo Motors needs a bit of lady luck. Could Sabrina oblige?

Money Monthly

INFLATION AND UNEMPLOYMENT

The latest official statistics on the economy give little comfort to the Government. Inflation rose by 10.2% during the past 12 months compared with a rise of 9.6% for the previous year. Logo now has a rate of inflation which is higher than most countries in the region.

Unemployment has also risen sharply. The latest figure is 981,000 which represents 13.5% of the total workforce. This is an increase of more than 120,000 compared with 12 months ago. One in five of the unemployed are school leavers unable to get jobs.

The only good news for the Government is in exports and productivity. Exports increased by nearly 5% last year, possibly due to the greater efforts by manufacturers to export more goods in the face of declining markets at home. Imports did not increase significantly, which meant that there was a slight surplus in the balance of payments compared with a slight deficit last year, but this may have been due to the closure of some of the more inefficient companies. The figure of gross production, however, shows a fall of 5.2% which reflects the present troubled state of the economy, particularly in the manufacturing sector.

While there is nothing unexpected in these latest statistics they confirm that the recession is serious and is likely to continue for some time, whatever measures might be taken to boost the economy.

OUTERWORLD TRADE

Facilitator's notes

Skills: production decisions, bargaining, trading, interviewing.
Time: 2–3 hours, including briefing and debriefing.
Numbers: 12–36 participants. There are six teams representing the five planets plus the media. With more than say 20 participants there can be an extra (seventh) team representing Outerworld Bank. Note that the simulation requires five planets, it will not work with four planets.
Photocopy: One copy of Notes for Participants for each participant. One copy of Economics Association statement for each team. Six copies of the FPBO memo for the broadcasters (they hand out five copies). One copy of their own memo for each of the five government teams. One or two copies of each of the five Commodity Tokens Sheets, perhaps with differently coloured paper for each commodity.
Optional stage 2: 6–7 copies of the Bank's Precious Metal Standard.
Optional stage 3: 6–7 copies of the Bank's Currency Exchange Rates.
Metal and exchange tokens for stages 2 and 3 might be produced and signed by Bank officials.
Materials and facilities: Scrap paper. If only one room is available the teams should be as far apart as possible. The Commodity Token Sheets should be cut out. The broadcasters should have a studio (see pages 29–30) and the facilitator (or Outerworld Bank) should have a base for keeping and handing out the commodity tokens.
Preliminary: Before the briefing, work out the mechanism for handing out tokens. If Aratba decides to abandon textiles and concentrate the extra 100 million Arats entirely on minerals they should be given six tokens of minerals (20 million Arats plus 100 million which equals six units) together with one token each for agriculture, engineering and chemicals, with the nine tokens totalling 300 million Arats in value. Tokens should always equal the total value given on each team's memo.
Briefing: The time limits for (a) planning (b) trading and (c) broadcasts are probably best left flexible, but could start with a tentative 5–10 minutes allowed for each period.
Action: Stage by stage. After each complete round (year) collect all tokens; they cannot be saved, they are consumed. Stages 2 and 3 are optional — they demonstrate the benefits of abandoning barter. When the participants have become familiar with the mechanism it is possible to introduce (invent) a production failure in a country, or inflation, which leads to crisis management, economic disruption, political implications, and problems for broadcasters.
Debriefing: It may be a good idea to let each team debrief themselves and set an agenda for a joint discussion. As well as lessons about international trade the discussion could cover economic and political initiatives, broadcasting presentation, and group dynamics.

OUTERWORLD TRADE

Notes for participants

Roles
1. Planetary Government Ministers (five governments)
2. Planetary TV/radio reporters

Documents
1. Statement by Outerworld Economics Association
2. Confidential documents for Governments
3. A memo for the broadcasters
4. Commodity tokens for trading

Situation
The five planets of Outerworld each produce for internal consumption the same five major commodities. The five governments have jointly agreed to all the points of a statement by the Outerworld Economics Association and are to start interplanetary trade.

Events
There are successive periods for (a) planning production, (b) trading, and (c) broadcasts. During the planning stage the governments take plans to the facilitator and receive commodity tokens equal to the total currency value of their production/consumption. Changes in production must be in whole units. Tokens must be handed back each year because they have been consumed. The saving of tokens is impossible. Trading is by interplanetary visits of trade delegations.

Conditions
You must behave with professional intent, which includes bearing in mind the interests of your planet (or TV organization). If you wish to order anything apart from changing production the consequences are decided by facilitator, perhaps after consultation. Thus, if you ordered a war the order could be disobeyed and you might be arrested.

You must not invent 'facts' to win arguments, but you can invent details if they are plausible and consistent with the documents.

You can do anything you have not been told not to do, but you must accept your roles and professional responsibilities.

Outerworld Economics Association

The Outerworld Economics Association has passed the following five-part resolution:

1. We declare unanimously in favour of introducing interplanetary trade.

2. We urge all five Planetary Governments to abandon production of goods which they find difficult or expensive and switch production to goods which are easier to produce.

3. Although a planet could suffer an economic disaster if it stopped producing a particular commodity and then failed to receive that particular commodity in trading, we believe this can be avoided by prudent economic planning and friendly negotiation.

4. Any managerial or personnel problems which result from switching production can be alleviated if the Five Planets Broadcasting Organisation uses its influence to highlight the long established interplanetary culture of job-switching, attachments, flexible job training, and job appreciation attitudes.

5. We urge that the broadcasts be held after each round of trading and that these broadcasts be deemed Essential Broadcasts under Section 32a and 32b of Interplanetary Law:

> Section 32.
> a. Essential broadcasts are those broadcasts which are deemed essential by prior joint agreement between the governments of the five planets.
>
> b. All Government Ministers are required to give undivided attention to essential broadcasts. Ministers who fail to do so will be prosecuted under Section 45 of the Act dealing with Subversive Interplanetary Conduct and will be liable to fines and/or dismissal from office.

Aratba

MEMO

The Ministry of Trade supplies the following information, as requested.

The cost of one year's production of 'yearly consumption units' is:

Yearly consumption (and production)	Commodities/goods	Cost in Arats (millions)
1 unit	Minerals	20
1 unit	Agriculture	40
1 unit	Engineering	60
1 unit	Chemicals	80
1 unit	Textiles	100
5 units	Total production/consumption	300

Brinland

MEMO

The Ministry of Trade supplies the following information, as requested.

The cost of one year's production of 'yearly consumption units' is:

Yearly consumption (and production)	Commodities/goods	Cost in Brins (millions)
1 unit	Textiles	2
1 unit	Minerals	4
1 unit	Agriculture	6
1 unit	Engineering	8
1 unit	Chemicals	10
5 units	Total production/consumption	30

Camgal

MEMO

The Ministry of Trade supplies the following
information, as requested.

The cost of one year's production of 'yearly
consumption units' is:

Yearly consumption (and production)	Commodities/goods	Cost in Cams (millions)
1 unit	Chemicals	10
1 unit	Textiles	20
1 unit	Minerals	30
1 unit	Agriculture	40
1 unit	Engineering	50
5 units	Total production/consumption	150

Denway

MEMO

The Ministry of Trade supplies the following information, as requested.

The cost of one year's production of 'yearly consumption units' is:

Yearly consumption (and production)	Commodities/goods	Cost in Dens (millions)
1 unit	Engineering	1
1 unit	Chemicals	2
1 unit	Textiles	3
1 unit	Minerals	4
1 unit	Agriculture	5
5 units	Total production/consumption	15

ESTIL

MEMO

The Ministry of Trade supplies the following information, as requested.

The cost of one year's production of 'yearly consumption units' is:

Yearly consumption (and production)	Commodities/goods	Cost in Ests (millions)
1 unit	Agriculture	100
1 unit	Engineering	200
1 unit	Chemicals	300
1 unit	Textiles	400
1 unit	Minerals	500
5 units	Total production/consumption	1500

Five Planets Broadcasting Organization

Memo – Essential Broadcasts

From   FPBO Management
To   Essential Broadcasts Unit

Please inform immediately the Ministers of all five governments of the following arrangements for the official broadcasts. The statement is to be released to the media later today.

FPBO has pleasure in announcing a series of 5 minute Essential Broadcasts to be entitled 'Outerworld Trade'. These will deal exclusively with news and comments arising out of inter-planetary trade.

FPBO will extend any of the Essential Broadcasts to 10 minutes if so requested by the Five Governments before the end of any trading period.

FPBO has editorial control of all Essential Broadcasts. It aims to provide as full and fair a coverage as possible. Some of these broadcasts may consist entirely of news items. Others might included interviews with ministers.

FPBO is responsible for ensuring that no broadcast exceeds its 5 minute (or 10 minute) duration even if this means terminating an interview abruptly.

OUTERWORLD BANK

Precious Metal Standard

In order to overcome some of the difficulties caused by barter arrangements and the fact that individual currencies are not acceptable for large business transactions outside their own planets the Central Banks of the Five Planets have agreed and jointly funded a Precious Metal Standard (PMS) which will be administered free of charge by Outerworld Bank in order to provide an acceptable interplanetary currency.

At any time of trading Outerworld Bank will buy or sell units of Precious Metals (PMs) in exchange for individual planetary currencies, as follows:

PMs (units)	Arats (millions)	Brins (millions)	Cams (millions)	Dens (millions)	Ests (millions)
1	20	2	10	1	100
2	40	4	20	2	200
3	60	6	30	3	300
4	80	8	40	4	400
5	100	10	50	5	500

OUTERWORLD BANK

Currency Exchange Credit Transactions

The Central Banks of the five planets have agreed to abandon the Precious Metal Standard and institute exchange credit transactions which should allow individual planets to deal with interplanetary trade more easily. The five Central Banks are jointly funding the exchange system.

Outerworld Bank will fix the exchange rate each year to regulate the currency transactions, and will act in the roles of consultants and observers.

The first interplanetary currency rate is fixed as follows:

$$1 \text{ Den} = 2 \text{ Brins} = 10 \text{ Cams} = 20 \text{ Arats} = 100 \text{ Ests}$$

MINERALS ONE UNIT	MINERALS ONE UNIT	MINERALS TWO UNITS
MINERALS ONE UNIT	MINERALS ONE UNIT	MINERALS TWO UNITS
MINERALS ONE UNIT	MINERALS ONE UNIT	MINERALS TWO UNITS
MINERALS ONE UNIT	MINERALS ONE UNIT	MINERALS TWO UNITS
MINERALS ONE UNIT	MINERALS ONE UNIT	MINERALS TWO UNITS

80 *The ten simulations*

AGRICULTURE ONE UNIT	**AGRICULTURE ONE UNIT**	**AGRICULTURE TWO UNITS**
AGRICULTURE ONE UNIT	**AGRICULTURE ONE UNIT**	**AGRICULTURE TWO UNITS**
AGRICULTURE ONE UNIT	**AGRICULTURE ONE UNIT**	**AGRICULTURE TWO UNITS**
AGRICULTURE ONE UNIT	**AGRICULTURE ONE UNIT**	**AGRICULTURE TWO UNITS**
AGRICULTURE ONE UNIT	**AGRICULTURE ONE UNIT**	**AGRICULTURE TWO UNITS**

ENGINEERING ONE UNIT	ENGINEERING ONE UNIT	ENGINEERING TWO UNITS
ENGINEERING ONE UNIT	ENGINEERING ONE UNIT	ENGINEERING TWO UNITS
ENGINEERING ONE UNIT	ENGINEERING ONE UNIT	ENGINEERING TWO UNITS
ENGINEERING ONE UNIT	ENGINEERING ONE UNIT	ENGINEERING TWO UNITS
ENGINEERING ONE UNIT	ENGINEERING ONE UNIT	ENGINEERING TWO UNITS

82 *The ten simulations*

CHEMICALS ONE UNIT	***CHEMICALS ONE UNIT***	***CHEMICALS TWO UNITS***
CHEMICALS ONE UNIT	***CHEMICALS ONE UNIT***	***CHEMICALS TWO UNITS***
CHEMICALS ONE UNIT	***CHEMICALS ONE UNIT***	***CHEMICALS TWO UNITS***
CHEMICALS ONE UNIT	***CHEMICALS ONE UNIT***	***CHEMICALS TWO UNITS***
CHEMICALS ONE UNIT	***CHEMICALS ONE UNIT***	***CHEMICALS TWO UNITS***

TEXTILES ONE UNIT	TEXTILES ONE UNIT	TEXTILES TWO UNITS
TEXTILES ONE UNIT	TEXTILES ONE UNIT	TEXTILES TWO UNITS
TEXTILES ONE UNIT	TEXTILES ONE UNIT	TEXTILES TWO UNITS
TEXTILES ONE UNIT	TEXTILES ONE UNIT	TEXTILES TWO UNITS
TEXTILES ONE UNIT	TEXTILES ONE UNIT	TEXTILES TWO UNITS

84 *The ten simulations*

PEG SPOTTING

Facilitator's notes

Skills: personal relationships, flexibility, insights, assessments.
Time: 1 1/2 – 2 hours, including briefing and debriefing, perhaps longer if there are more than 20 participants.
Numbers: 12 or more participants. With 12 there could be 4 assessors and four groups of 2 trainees, with 20 there could be 4 assessors and four groups of 4 trainees, with more than 20 have eight tables (two tables for each task).
Photocopying: One copy of Notes for Participants for each participant. One copy of How to Take the Tests and Before Test and After Test forms for each participant (the assessors have these for reference only). One copy of How to Assess the Tests for each assessor. Also one or two copies of the one-word Instructions (for the assessors).
Materials and facilities: Blank name tags for each participant. Four (or eight) separate tables for the tests, with one envelope for each table to contain the Instruction for that table. Plain paper (A4 size is suitable), pens, paper clips, elastic bands.
Briefing: Discuss time limits and furniture. If only one room is available then the trainees could go out into the corridor a few minutes before they are due for their tests. It is not a good idea to allow more than say 10–15 minutes between receiving the documents and starting the tests, otherwise the trainees will have filled in their forms and be waiting around. The assessors can always refer back to their forms when the testing starts. Do not, of course, reveal what the four Instructions are.
Action: Make sure that the assessors have been provided with sufficient materials — paper, paper clips, pens, elastic bands. A plentiful supply of paper is particularly important since these sheets will get used up, folded or torn during each test and need replacing.
Debriefing: There is a good case for deferring the main part of the debriefing to allow time for the facilitator to assimilate what the trainees wrote in their Before Test and After Test forms — a tea break might be sufficient for this purpose. Allow time for participants to reveal what happened in the counselling sessions. It is important that the ex-trainees should be given the opportunity of saying what they thought about the assessors and the counselling they received.

PEG SPOTTING

Notes for participants

Roles
1. Assessors in the Ministry of Careers
2. Trainees on the staff of the Ministry of Careers

Documents
1. Before Test and After Test forms for comments by trainees
2. How to Take the Tests. Instructions for trainees
3. How to Assess the Tests. Instructions for assessors
4. One-sentence Instructions for use during tests

Situation
In the Republic of Logo the Government's huge Ministry of Careers helps to select people for jobs, including jobs in the Careers Ministry itself. Early in their course at the Ministry the trainees have a group assessment followed by counselling. The assessors do not award marks or grade the trainees, they just note what happens and use the examples in later counselling sessions. The purpose is not to fit the trainees into specific jobs — clerical, management, design — but to discuss broad areas — creativity, organization, personal relationships. No decisions are made, only notes for future guidance.

Events
The simulation begins with the assessors and trainees meeting separately. While the assessors familiarize themselves with the assessment system the trainees fill in the Before Test comments form. During the assessment there will be a time limit for tasks, and then each group moves clockwise to the next table. After each table has been visited the trainees withdraw and write their After Test comments while the assessors discuss their observations. The final stage is the counselling.

Conditions
You must behave with professional intent. You must not invent 'facts' to enhance your own position, but you can invent peripheral details provided they are plausible and consistent with the materials.

You can do anything you have not been told not to do, but you must accept your roles and responsibilities.

For Assessors. Confidential

How to assess the tests

1. First fill in your name tag. Use only your first name, or a shortened version of it.

2. Arrange the four tables so as to make it easy for the trainees to move clockwise from one to another.

3. On each table place an envelope containing one of the four instruction words — Construct, Classify, Design, Communicate. Also place half a dozen or so sheets of clean unused paper, a few pens, a handful of paper clips and a few elastic bands on each table. The precise number of each does not matter but if they get used up (written on, bent, broken) then they should be replaced by an equal number of items before the next group moves to that table.

4. Set a time limit, about 5 minutes, for each assignment, and you can give a one-minute warning to the trainees before the time is up.

5. Each table has its own assessor who does not move from table to table, but who watches four groups each do the same task. Assessors must not give hints. If someone says 'Are we allowed to bend the paper clips' then do not say 'You can bend the paper clips if you wish to do so' but reply 'I cannot answer questions. My job is only to observe'.

6. When the time has expired, say 'Stop'. (See instructions to trainees.) After you have replaced any used up materials, say 'Move'.

7. Do not award marks or grades or try to decide who is 'best'. Simply observe (and make notes of) what actually happens — who does what, who says what. For example:
   (a) Do they obey the instructions?
   (b) Do they cooperate?
   (c) What ideas do they have?
   (d) What initiatives do they show?
   (e) Anything that is unusual or interesting.

8. How you conduct the counselling session is up to you but the starting point could be what you observed in the tests. The sole purpose is to discover useful information about people's behaviour — how they organize themselves or each other, their attitudes to colleagues, their ambitions. Remember that you are assessors of people, not appointments boards. You are not trying to find jobs for the trainees. All that comes next month.

Form: MC.007786.A

How to take the tests

1. First fill in your name tag. Use only your first name, or a shortened version of it.

2. Fill in the Before Test form. You are asked to talk about your personal feelings about taking tests. It is in your own interests to be honest.

3. When you enter the assessment room the assessors will divide you up into groups and you sit at four tables. Each table will contain some sheets of paper, pens, paper clips and elastic bands. There will also be an envelope containing a one-word instruction. You must not open the envelope until the assessors tell you to do so.

4. When you see the instruction you may wonder what it has to do with the materials on the table. That is your problem. What, if anything, you do with the materials is up to you.

5. When the assessors say 'Stop' then that means stop immediately and replace the instruction in its envelope.

6. When the assessors say 'Move' then move immediately in a clockwise direction to the next table.

7. After visiting all four tables you will be asked to return to the waiting room to fill in the After Test form in which you describe your feelings about your experiences at the four tables.

8. Finally, in the counselling session you will be meeting the assessors individually or in groups to discuss how you coped with the tasks. Do not hesitate to tell them what you think; their purpose at this stage is not to find you jobs, but to get to know you better and help you.

Form MC.0899.T

Before test

My name is ....

My personal feelings about taking tests are as follows:

Form MC.0900.T

After test

My name is ....

My personal feelings about taking these four tests are as follows:

Form MC.0901.T

The instruction for the group at this table is:

Design

Design: To sketch, to plan, to make a drawing for some construction, to fashion, to create a work.
(Logon National Dictionary)

The instruction for the group at this table is:

Classify

Classify: To arrange, to sort out, to distribute into classes, to sort into groups according to some system.
(Logon National Dictionary)

The Instruction for the group at this table is:

Construct

Construct: To build, to make, to fit together, to place parts together, to form, to assemble into a whole.
(Logon National Dictionary)

The instruction for the group at this table is:

Communicate

Communicate: To impart information, to tell, to discuss, to engage in interactive behaviour.
(Logon National Dictionary)

FORT

Facilitator's notes

Skills: evaluation, planning, strategy, design, decision making.

Time: 1 – 2 hours, including briefing and debriefing.

Numbers: 6-30 participants. Adjust the roles and size of groups according to overall numbers. There should not be more than five in a group. With more than 20 participants the War Lord can have one or two assistants, and there can be Captains of Spies, Arms, Food, Warriors and even religious leaders.

Photocopying: One copy of Notes for Participants for everyone. The War Lord and other leaders should each have a copy of the map and the intelligence. Groups of planners/architects should each have one or two copies of the two documents.

Materials and facilities: Several coins of same denomination (1p or 1 cent are suitable) representing 100 paces. Plain paper, scrap paper, rulers, pens.

Briefing: Routine.

Action: Straightforward

Debriefing: There is no 'right' answer regarding the siting of the fort. The high ground to the north is suitable for defence but it is some way from the building material (wood), it is beyond arrow range of Blood Ford and could be cut off from supplies from the south. Other options are to site the fort immediately north or south of the ford but these would be more vulnerable to attack since they would not be on high ground. The design of the interior of the fort is really a matter of opinions and priorities — should it include stables, a place of worship, officers' quarters? As with the other simulations the debriefing should not try to determine a 'right' answer but look for management qualities — the group dynamics, the effectiveness of the presentation, the willingness to see other people's points of view and whether the different groups tried to 'win' irrespective of the merits of the case, or whether they took an overall view (corporate as distinct from departmental) and gave priority to the needs of the liberation army.

FORT

Notes for participants

Roles
War Lord, and several groups of planners/architects. If there are sufficient numbers there can be Captains of Spies, Arms, etc.

Documents
Map of area near Blood Ford and Intelligence document from the Captain of Spies. You may also have a coin to help you to work out distances and design the fort to size.

Situation
It is 2000 years ago and you are are trying to liberate your country from a foreign tyrant. Six months ago your warriors suffered a heavy defeat as they retreated southwards across Blood Ford. Your Army has been reformed and is moving north towards the ford and is one day's march away. Your War Lord has approved all three suggestions in the last part of the report from the Captain of Spies.

Events
The War Lord (and any Captains) will divide the planners into groups, explain anything that needs explaining, and set a time limit for the urgent task of designing a fort. When the time limit expires the different groups will assemble before the War Lord and explain, advocate, and discuss the designs.

Conditions
You must behave with professional intent.

You cannot invent 'facts' in order to enhance your plan. You cannot invent weapons that are superior to bows and arrows, or claim that your fort could be built in 20 minutes, or claim to know more than is revealed in the intelligence document. You can invent plausible details so long as they are consistent with the documents.

Providing you are loyal to your country you can do anything you have not been told not to do, but if you issue orders then it is up to the facilitator to decide the consequences of those orders.

FROM THE CAPTAIN OF SPIES

Intelligence from Blood Ford

FIVE of our spies crossed Blood Ford and went north for half a day and found no enemy. Friendly shepherds said that the army of the tyrant is in Capital City three days to the north and that it be near 10,000 warriors with some 200 horse warriors.

ALTHOUGH our Army be but 7,000 warriors and 150 horse warriors our bows shoot true for 40 paces and 100 paces overall. The bows of the enemy shoot true for only 20 paces and 50 paces overall.

SOUTH of the ford are two thick woods with trees in plenty for building, for weapons and for fires. The hill to the north rises to 400 paces higher than the river, with a steep slope on the north side. It is the only hill nearby. There are no trees on the hill but there are stones and boulders. The river east and west of the ford is narrow and swift flowing. There are stones nearby.

WE have food enough from lands to the south and sturdy wagons that can cross the ford, but there is little food in the barren lands northwards to Capital City.

Herein are our prayers and pleas

WE do humbly suggest, plead and pray that a fort should be built near Blood Ford to protect our advance, and so help the gods to favour our just and noble cause.

WE do humbly suggest, plead and pray that our council do severally divide and in groups do make designs for a fort, with space and provision within for all that may be needed therein, and do then plead, talk, and compare the plans.

WE do humbly suggest, plead and pray that the fort be not larger than one hundred paces across, and may be smaller, but be so built of wood and stones as to form a defence, a refuge, and a place of secure supply for our army.

May the gods be with us in our work.

FORT 95

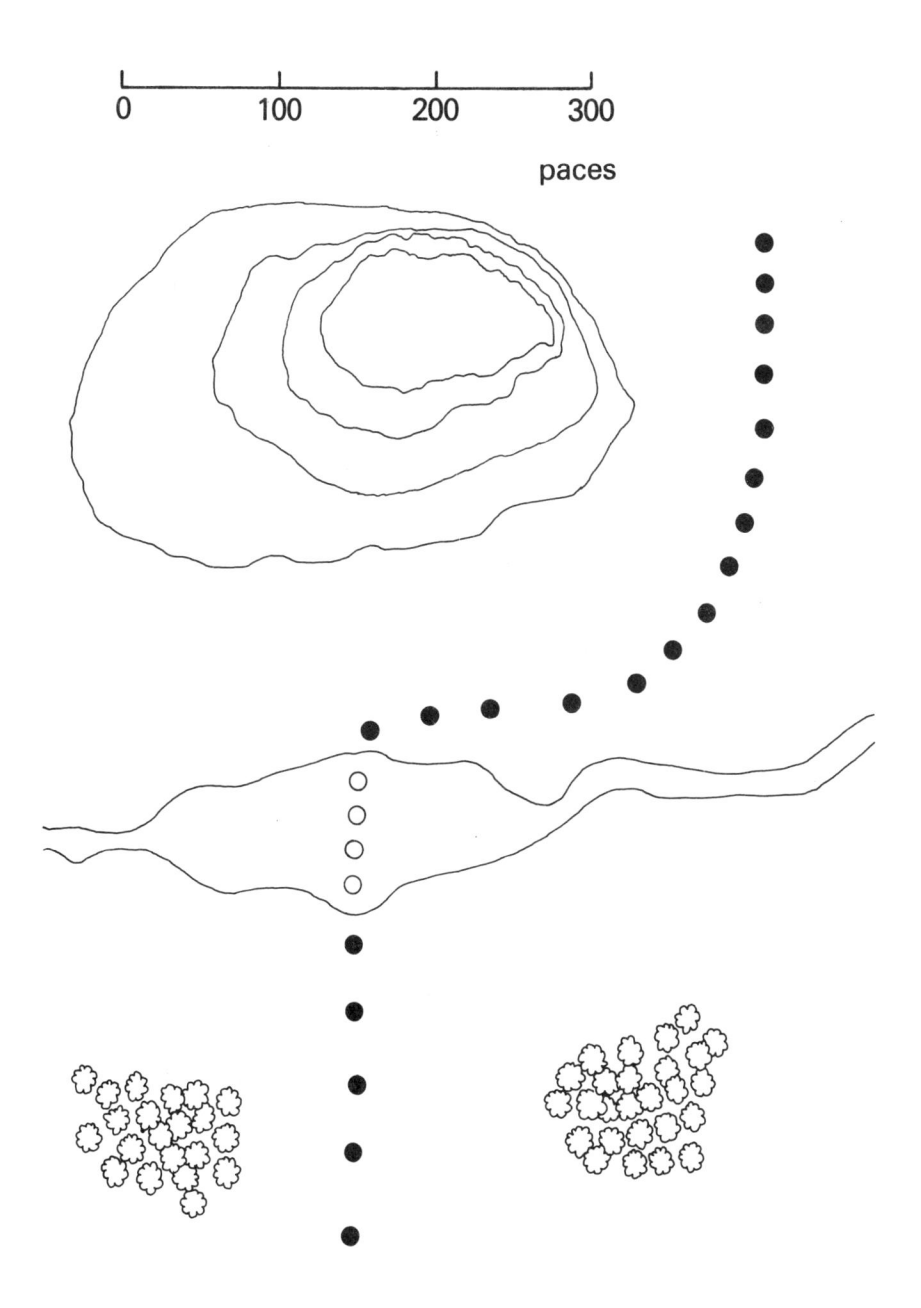

```
    0    100   200   300
              paces
```

LINK MANAGEMENT

Facilitator's notes

Skills: organization, planning, design, manufacture, entertainment.
Time: 1½ – 2 hours, including briefing and debriefing.
Numbers: 10 – 50 participants. With only 10 the entertainment companies can be reduced to two with 4 participants in each (boss, manager and two workers) plus two participants representing Logon International Top Hotels (LITH). With large numbers there can be 10 or more in each of the four entertainment companies with the LITH team increased proportionally.
Photocopying: One for each participant of Notes for Participants and the LITH Simsheet.
Materials and facilities: Each of the entertainment companies will require white and coloured paper, glue, scissors, rulers and coloured pens, and scrap paper. A few large cards could be added — it should not be spelled out that they could be used for posters, advertising (etc) as one of the optional activities mentioned in the LITH Simsheet. If the cards are queried by LITH team then they are 'available material'; if queried by any of the four entertainment companies then give the standard 'I'm not really here' reply. An additional touch of realism (and a mark of ownership) would be to produce company labels to place on each group's tables, including one for the LITH team. Two rooms would be better than one. If only one room is available then perhaps the entertainment companies can wait in a corridor until LITH has arranged the furniture, distributed the materials to the tables, etc.
Briefing: Routine, expect perhaps to emphasize that the organization is the job of the LITH team.
Action: Avoid giving hints. If LITH team ask you 'Shall we place the tables like this?' or 'Should we mark each team so many out of 10?' then explain that you are not present. In observing the event it is worth noting (surreptitiously) whether the bosses restrict their visits to the workers to two visits of no more than 2 minutes each or whether they exceed the time limit even if only by a few seconds, and also whether the LITH team are also observing this.
Debriefing: It can be useful if everyone remains in their groups and debriefs themselves and perhaps set the agenda for the main debriefing. Subsequent discussion can cover the value of using simulations in the awarding of contracts in certain cases, of the relationships between management and staff, of communication skills, and perhaps the use of drama, humour and entertainment for promotion, explanation and publicity.

LINK MANAGEMENT

Notes for participants

Roles
1. Executives of Logon International Top Hotels (LITH)
2. Representatives of Bright Amusements, Entertainments Incorporated, Fun and Games, The Novelty Company.

Documents
LITH Simsheet (for all participants). Paper, glue, pens, etc.

Situation
The main hotel chain in the Republic of Logo (Logon International Top Hotels) is planning to introduce Novelty Weekends at various hotels to attract children and their parents. They have invited four entertainment companies — who make paper hats, organize children's parties — to participate in a simulation for the purposes of deciding who should be awarded the contract(s). The four entertainment companies have all agreed to this procedure.

Events
The event starts with the entertainment companies meeting separately, but allowed to talk to each other if they wish, having just received the LITH Simsheet. The LITH team, meanwhile, have the job of organizing the furniture in the Simroom and distributing the production materials. The second stage is that the LITH team welcome the entertainment companies into the Simroom and explain anything that seems appropriate — time limits, additional facilities, etc. After the production run the LITH team will be expected to announce their findings.

Conditions
You must behave with professional intent, which means bearing in mind what you hope for your future career.

You must not invent facts to win a contract — 'Our company has received the top design award for the past three years.'

You can do anything you have not been told not to do, providing you accept your roles and responsibilities.

LINK MANAGEMENT 99

LITH SIMSHEET

Welcome to our simulation. Thank you for coming.

We are satisfied that all four companies have facilities for organising Novelty Weekends, so we are trying to find out how each company can work together as a team, how well you cope with difficulties in carrying out the tasks, and what sort of ideas you produce. We apologise for the somewhat unrealistic rules about who can visit whom in the production lines. However, the rules are not intended to imitate a normal production line but to see how you tackle communication problems and how well you obey the instructions on this sheet.

Roles: Whatever might be your position in your Company we ask you to allocate one person for the role of boss, one for the role of manager, and the others in the role of workers.

Organisation: You will have a strip of territory representing a production line with the boss at one end, the workers at the other, and the manager in between.

1. The workers are not permitted to visit the manager or the boss, they must remain where they are.

2. The manager can visit the workers or the boss at any time.

3. The boss can visit the manager at any time, but can visit the workers on no more than two occasions, each visit lasting no more than 2 minutes.

Tasks: 1. To design and construct one (and only one) attractive and amusing paper chain which must not fall apart when held up by one end.

2. To present your chain and explain your ideas.

Materials: White and coloured paper, glue, scissors, coloured pens, scrap paper, etc.

Time: Before you begin you will be given a time limit to complete your production chains.

Options: How you divide the work is up to you. Provided you obey the above instructions you can do anything that seems suitable in the circumstances. There is nothing to stop bosses from sacking workers, or to stop workers from going on strike. There is nothing to stop a team doing something in addition to making the paper chain - for example, drawing up plans about costs and publicity.

We hope you enjoy our simulation. Good luck.

COMPUTER WORLD

Facilitator's notes

Skills: confidentiality, diplomacy, subtlety, investigation, ethics.
Time: 1 ½ – 2 hours, including briefing and debriefing.
Numbers: The ideal number is 8 participants. With a few more than 8 there could be an extra Software Manufacturer and/or International Oil Company, or any role could have an assistant. With only 7 the International Oil role or the multinational finance role could be abandoned. With 14 and upwards there could be two (or more) separate events.
Photocopying: One copy of Notes for Participants for each participant. One copy of *Computers News and Views* for each participant. One copy of the role card sheet for each event. The role cards are intended to be small for easy concealment.
Materials and facilities: Prepare name and job tags (perhaps an art department could make them look official) and cut out the confidential role cards, which could be handed out in envelopes. There should be a chalkboard (flip-chart, word processor) for *Computer News and Views*. Scrap paper is essential (for notes, contracts, agreements). Some form of refreshment could add realism. Corridors, spare rooms, the canteen, could be used to ensure privacy. Telephones might be used.
Briefing: With adults it should be minimal and ultra cautious. With teenagers it can be useful to emphasize that they should start by standing up and moving around and that they should not form groups of more than say three people. With both adults and teenagers it could be profitable to rule (or discuss) whether eavesdropping in these circumstances is a criminal offence, or vaguely unethical, or fair game.
Action: Usually highly devious. Questions addressed to the facilitator might include 'Am I allowed to offer a bribe?' One answer could be 'Only by plausible amounts and only in Logon currency.' The fallback answer is the basic 'I don't know. I'm not really here'.
Debriefing: Since a great deal will have happened in private, the debriefing should last for at least half an hour in order to give people an opportunity to say what they did and why they did it. A good starting point is for each person to read out their role card. The debriefing could cover a host of related issues – efficient management of computer systems, ethics, the law, software piracy, hacking, confidentiality, espionage, security, diplomacy. One avenue is to speculate what might happen on the day after the event — arrests, writs, contracts, bankruptcy?

COMPUTER WORLD

Notes for participants

Roles
Executives, officials, experts and a journalist concerned with computers, security, hacking and fraud in the Republic of Logo.

Documents
1. Confidential individual role cards
2. *Computer News and Views*
3. Name and job tags

Situation
The settings are any places that are appropriate for meetings in pairs — computer exhibitions, receptions, restaurants, washrooms. There is a display board representing *Computer News and Views* for news reports by the journalist(s). Also any participant can write in one or two lines of news or comments (or an advertisement) subject to the editorial approval of the journalist(s).

Events
There is no schedule of events, only a time limit. The emphasis is on secrecy and movement. Participants should begin by standing up and moving around, and should meet in pairs. Pairs who see that someone else is standing nearby wishing to speak to one of them should conclude their own meeting as quickly and as conveniently possible. Although meetings of groups larger than two are permitted, they should not occur very often.

Conditions
You must behave with professional intent according to your role and the information in your role card, which includes bearing in mind your future career.

You must not invent 'facts' to win arguments or to enhance your own position, but you can invent peripheral details provided they are plausible and consistent with the materials.

You can do anything you have not been told not to do.

Computer News and Views

LAW AND THE COMPUTER

The long-debated Government bill to increase penalties for computer software piracy, computer fraud, damage to software, and for hacking has now become law.

For the first time hacking itself, even without damage, piracy, or fraud, has become illegal and persons convicted are liable to fines or prison sentences of up to two months.

The Computer Protection, Privacy, Piracy and Hacking Act has been greeted as a modest step forward in curbing undesirable and illegal practices which has affected all large organizations and software manufacturers. However, critics point out that hackers are extremely difficult to catch, that some large organizations give a nod and a wink to computer espionage, that computer fraud is undoubtedly far more prevalent than most people realize, and that piracy of software is widespread even within some public bodies such as schools and colleges.

VIRUS ATTACK

Unconfirmed reports from a usually reliable source say that the main Army computer of a Middle East country was infected by a virus introduced by a person unknown. The virus (which was itself a program) distorted the output and finally printed the message 'You have lost all your bows and arrows'. According to the reports it took a week to rid the system of the virus.

Name Tag Information | Role Card

Name Tag Information	Role Card
Software Manufacturer	Sales have fallen because of piracy. Your legal advisers say it would probably be lawful under the new Act to build a virus into programs which would operate only when pirated. However, the virus could be used illegally to bug any programs. You have excellent facilities to build a virus.
Executive Multinational Finance	Your Group has given you a confidential assignment and substantial funds to do anything legal to safeguard the security of the Group's computer systems.
Executive Computer Experiments	Your company specializes in designing tailor-made programs which seek out any virus in large computer systems, plus making virus killer programs. Costs are high and estimates depend on the amount of work involved.
Journalist *Computer News and Views*	You have personally and secretly developed a smart virus which not only infects and damages the host programs but sniffs if an anti-virus probe is being used and moves temporarily to another location to avoid detection. This smart virus is probably illegal but could be highly valuable.
Official Defence Ministry	The Ministry has given you a confidential assignment and substantial funds to do anything legal to safeguard security of defence computer networks.
Consultant Professor Central University (Computer Division)	The University has asked you to see what can be done to safeguard the examinations and confidential records. Secretly you are a well paid industrial spy for the Defence Department of a friendly foreign country and you have power of recruitment.
Official Ministry of Trade	The Trade Ministry has asked you to look at ways of making its computer system more secure. Secretly you are also paid by the Ministry of Internal Security to look for defence and industrial spies and pass on the information. You can recruit informants.
Executive International Oil	Some of your company's highly secret research and development programs have apparently been hacked by rivals. The Board of Directors has asked you to take whatever action is desirable.

ROCK ISLAND

Facilitator's notes

Skills: preferences, planning, analysis, decision making, presentation.
Time: 1½ – 2 hours, including briefing and debriefing
Numbers: 6 – 20 participants. With 20-40 the event can be run in parallel.
Photocopying: One copy of Notes for Participants for each participant. One copy per participant of all the other documents, except for the citizens' role cards which are supplied as one copy for every 3 participants.
Materials and facilities: Sheets of ruled paper and scrap paper. If art materials are available they could be used for presentation purposes in the party political broadcasts. If video cameras and tape recorders are used the operators can be members of the TV organization.
Briefing: As well as the main briefing there can be a mini-briefing before stages 2 and 3. In briefing the final stage it is important to emphasize that there is no studio audience, so the viewers should keep quiet, and not murmur, laugh, or applaud.
Action: If the above suggestion for three briefings is adopted then this will provide the breaks needed for changing the furniture arrangements. The first stage involves three groups (three cities), the second stage is a committee meeting of everyone (although subcommittees could be formed), and the third stage involves television studio arrangements. (See pages 29–30 for advice on TV studios.)
Debriefing: Unlike the other simulations, there are three separate but related occurrences. The decisions about citizens' preferences made during the first stage affect the analysis (traffic bottlenecks?) and recommendations of the second stage. These in turn provide facts which can be used in the party political broadcasts. It could be a good idea to ask each of the final groups — the political parties — to debrief themselves, including setting an agenda for the main debriefing as suggested for some of the earlier simulations.

The topics covered can include aspects from each of the three stages — the economics of sudden wealth, the problems of road transport, the political implications and the use of the media to put over policies and ideas. There are also the broader questions of group dynamics, managerial techniques, communication skills, and the use of effective and appropriate language.

ROCK ISLAND

Notes for participants

Roles
Stage 1. citizens
Stage 2. Transport Ministry officials
Stage 3. politicians

Documents
1. Transport questionnaire
2. *Home and Holiday Guide*
3. Role cards for citizens in the three main towns
4. Internal memo: Transport Ministry
5. *Rock Island Informant*

Situation
Rock Island, a poor country with a primitive transport system, discovered off-shore oil ten years ago. Almost everyone lives in the towns of Cap, Skur or Harb.

The Government has used the oil revenues to boost industry, to build motorways linking the towns, to build new towns and holiday centres and encourage people to move out of the slums, and to provide cars. A questionnaire has asked people for their preferences. An election is pending.

Events
Filling in a questionnaire, assessing the results, giving party political broadcasts.

Conditions
You must behave with professional intent in the three different roles — as citizens with family responsibilities, as government administrators, and as politicians.

You must not invent 'facts' to win arguments or to enhance your positions, but you can invent peripheral details if they are plausible and consistent with the facts in the materials.

You can do anything you have not been told not to do, but you must accept your roles and your responsibilities.

Transport questionnaire

- You have been chosen to take part in the Transport Survey.
- As you know, the Government has almost completed two new towns for living — Pinetops and Meadows. The rents are low and the accommodation is good. People who decide to move to new homes in Meadows or Pinetops will be entitled to a free small car, and six months' allocation of fuel, or the equivalent in money. Holidays taken in Adventureland or Golden Beach will be subsidized by the Government. It is all part of the plan to improve the quality of life in Rock Island.
- Before you fill in the questionnaire please look at the Home and Holiday Guide.
- All you have to do is to write on the dotted line the name of one of the towns marked in brackets after each question.

---

1. In which town do you work?

(Cap, Skur or Harb) ....

2. Where would you prefer to live?

(Pinetops or Meadows)..

3. Which holiday centre do you prefer?

(Adventureland or Golden Beach) ....

110 *The ten simulations*

Home and Holiday Guide

This guide has been produced by the Ministry of Transport to help you to choose which new town you would like move to, and which holiday centre you prefer. The new motorways make it easy to travel — with less than half an hour between towns. Even the journey from Cap to Pinetops takes only 25 minutes. The days of donkey travel and slums will soon be over.

Meadows New Town
Rivers, woods
Community centres
University
Shops, schools etc

Pinetops New Town
Mountains, lakes
Conference centres
Large hospital
Shops, schools etc

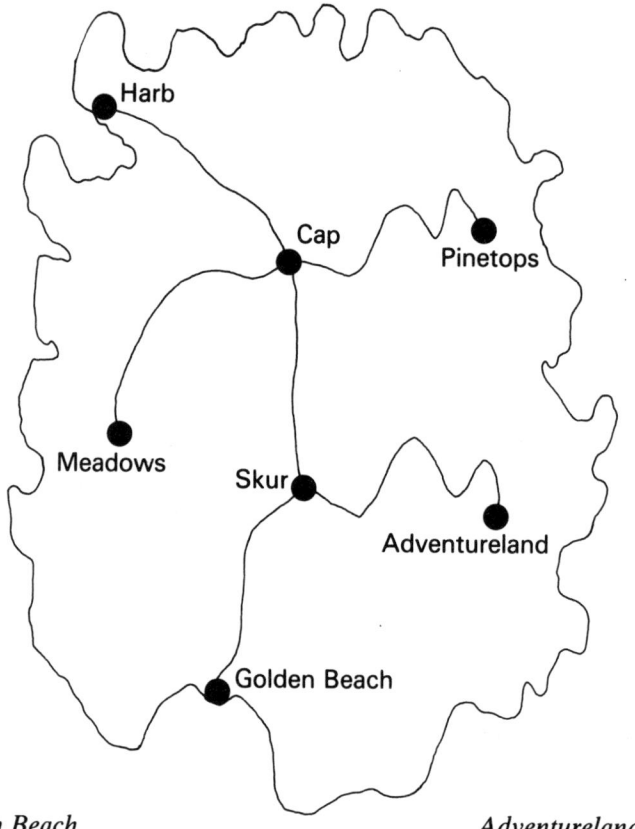

Rock Island

Golden Beach
Fabulous golden sands
Discos
A fun-packed holiday

Adventureland
Sporting centre
Pop and classical concerts
Comradeship

Role Card Citizen A

I live and work at Harb.

It is an old fishing town which has now been spoiled by oil installations.

My family do not like living in Harb and want to move.

Role Card Citizen B

I live and work in Skur.

It is the old agricultural centre which has been ruined by the uncontrolled growth of industries and there is a good deal of industrial pollution.

My family do not like living in Skur and want to move.

Role Card Citizen C

I live and work in Cap.

Cap is the capital and oldest city. It has been spoilt. The development of industrialization, transportation, hotels and official buildings has led to a rapid exodus of people from the centre into the suburbs and a shanty town on the outskirts is growing rapidly as people from Skur and Harb are attracted to the capital.

My family do not like living in Cap and want to move.

Ministry of Transport

Memorandum

From: Head of Administration

To: Questionnaire Report Staff

* Categorise the results of the survey in whatever way appears to be the most appropriate.

Included in your figures must be the estimated future traffic density for each of the 7 individual towns as related to (a) commuter traffic and (b) holiday traffic. The basis for the traffic density figures can be compiled from the questionnaire by adding up the numbers of

   (1) departures
   (2) arrivals
   (3) (wherever appropriate) through-traffic

In working out the estimates of future traffic density you can assume that with a population totalling nearly one million there will be about 100,000 cars on the roads each day.

* You are not restricted to dealing only with traffic density in towns. If you wish to produce other figures from the replies to the questionnaire then do so. You may draw whatever conclusions you wish and make any recommendations that seem suitable.

* The only restraint is that you must not venture into the political arena. Your conclusions and recommendations must relate solely to the transport situation. It may be that some politicians will make use of your report for political purposes, but if you stick to the facts and use neutral language then we will be in a position to defend ourselves against criticism.

Rock Island Informant

ELECTION HEAT

All three parties make their final election broadcast tonight. They will draw lots to decide in which order the broadcasts should take place.

Our political correspondent says that the Government's Forward Party is likely to argue that although there have been serious problems in changing from poverty to wealth the lessons are being learned and the Forward Party is the best suited to lead Rock Island into a challenging future.

The Land Party is likely to stress traditional values and the need for slowing down the changes which still remain part of the Forward Party's plans. It stresses the need for strong Government action to help agriculture and stringent controls on such questions as pollution, crime and corruption.

The Popular Party will undoubtedly attack the Government's record on industrialization and advocate a transfer of power to local committees to deal with abuses more quickly and more effectively as they arise.

Our correspondent says it will be interesting to see if at this last stage of the election the two opposition parties can state clearly what they would do about the Government's promises. So far neither the Land Party nor the Popular Party has spelt out whether or not they would honour the Government's promise of free cars, subsidized housing and holidays, and the removal of the slums.

SELLING THE FLAG

Facilitator's notes

Skills: evaluating, planning, interviewing, presentation, debating.
Time: 1½–3 hours, including briefing and debriefing.
Numbers: 10–25 participants. The participants can be divided equally into five groups representing the four political parties, plus Atlan TV.
Photocopying: One copy of Notes for Participants for each participant. Each political party and Atlan TV should have at least one copy of the Parliamentary Order Paper, the *Atlan Advocate* and *Outlook Atlantic*. One copy of the Atlan TV memo for each journalist.
Materials and facilities: If video cameras and tape recorders are used then they should be given to the TV team. There are three settings: private discussion rooms, the TV studio, and the debating chamber which should be a five-sided arrangement with the Chair (and perhaps assistant or secretary) occupying one of the sides. Name tags and Party labels could be helpful, particularly in the television interviewing. Ample scrap paper should be provided.
Briefing: Discuss the rules for private meetings — is eavesdropping permitted or illegal? Decide on whether the debate should have an unalterable time schedule or whether it could be changed as a result of negotiations between the politicians and the Chair. Discuss the number and timing of the broadcasts. There should be at least three — one before the debate, one during an adjournment, and one after the debate. Emphasize that all participants should watch TV broadcasts with undivided attention. (See pages 29–30 for advice on setting up a TV studio.)
Action: Routine. If the journalists are not in the studio a minute or two before transmission then do not warn them or draw their attention to the time. If they are not present at the start of transmission then tell them that another programme has replaced their broadcast and that the Editor of Newsprobe has ordered their instant dismissal. (They were warned in their memo.) Give them the role of observers, or messengers, or organizers, or politicians, and ask for volunteers from the political parties to take on the temporary job of interviewer(s) for subsequent broadcasts.
Debriefing: One option is to keep the participants in the final groups and debriefing themselves, and perhaps set the agenda for the general discussion. Since the environment in the simulation is the world of real superpowers the participants should be given the chance of disclaiming their own arguments in the debate — 'Although I argued in favour of selling out to country X what I really think is that....'

Discussion is likely to include the economic and political aspects of any government privatizing its services, industries, utilities. It should also cover general questions — public speaking, diplomacy, negotiations, communication skills.

SELLING THE FLAG

Notes for participants

Roles
1. Politicians of political parties Ai, Bee, Cee and Dee
2. Journalists on Atlan TV.

Documents
1. Parliamentary Order paper
2. *Atlan Advocate*
3. *Outlook Atlantic*
4. Atlan TV memo (for journalists only)

Situation
The mid-Atlantic country of Atlan has no government. An election has returned four parties in equal numbers. There will be a special parliamentary debate on the main election issue — the sale of Atlan.

Events
The four political parties and Atlan TV meet separately to discuss the arguments in favour of their proposals and to make arrangements for the broadcasts and for the debate. There will be at least three broadcasts — before the debate, during an adjournment, and after the debate.

Conditions
Any negotiations between parties or within parties can take place before the debate or during adjournments. The debate and the broadcasts must be given undivided attention by everyone.

You must behave with professional intent in your role and accept the basic point of view of your own Party (whatever your personal views might be). If you change your mind it should be only because of points made in the debate or during private negotiations.

You must not invent 'facts' to win arguments. For example, the reactions of any of the superpowers to the proposal are not known and must not be invented.

You can do anything you have not been told not to do.

Special debate

Atlan Assembly Order Paper

Special provisions for this debate have been agreed between the four parties. They are as follows:

1. A member of Dee Party will take the Chair, but will have no vote.

2. Each party will take it in turn to make an opening statement without discussion or interruption in support of their own motions, as follows:

> Ai Party: Atlan be sold to the United States on terms to be negotiated.
>
> Bee Party: Atlan be sold to the Soviet Union on terms to be negotiated.
>
> Cee Party: Atlan be sold to Western Europe on terms to be negotiated.
>
> Dee Party: Atlan be not sold.

3. The debate will then resume normally. It must not overrun the allotted time and the Chair has the responsibility and duty to announce and order 'The debate is now adjourned' before an adjournment and 'The debate is now closed' at the end of the debate.

4. At any time an adjournment will be called if requested by at least two political parties. Before the debate or during an adjournment the Chair will consult with the four parties and will decide on the order in which the proposals will be put to the vote.

5. Motions to amend any of the resolutions will be accepted by the Chair only if they were circulated in advance of that sitting and not if they were raised during that sitting.

6. For a proposal to be passed it must receive more than half of the votes of those who vote.

Atlan Advocate

The President's broadcast lasted just 2 minutes 7 seconds. Here is the full text:

As you all know, there is at present no Government in Atlan. The four parties have been returned in equal numbers in an election which was dominated by proposals that Atlan should be sold in order to rescue the country from bankruptcy. As a way forward in this difficult situation I have requested the Assembly to debate the four proposals as a first step in ending the damaging uncertainty at home and abroad.

The reason for speaking to you tonight is that I wish to say some words of reassurance about what the media have referred to as the 'Selling the flag' debate. I want to reassure you on two points.

Firstly, the debate is not to decide whether or not to sell our country — it is to decide which of the four questions should be put in a referendum. If none of the four proposals achieves a majority vote then the question in the referendum will be the one which receives the most votes. Thus, the final choice is in your hands. You will decide the issue in the referendum.

My second reassurance is that the three proposals for the sale all have an important proviso — that the terms must be negotiated. This means that unless the terms are acceptable to Atlan the sale will not take place. The three political parties which favour the sale — Ai, Bee and Cee — have all said that they wish to preserve our culture and our customs and our control over our own local affairs. In other words, Atlan will not lose its own identity, it will not be swallowed up by another country. If the sale goes ahead then it would be on terms which would improve the economic situation in Atlan. No other terms would be acceptable. I do not need to remind you of the huge national debt, of massive unemployment, of a very high rate of inflation, and shortages of many goods.

One final word. While I do not seek to bind the hands of any of our future negotiators I feel it would be wrong for Atlan to become the military base of a superpower. Atlan has no nuclear weapons, and I trust that no such weapons will ever be placed on our soil. I urge you, the people, to have faith in our democracy, faith in our culture, and faith in our future.

Outlook Atlantic

SELLING THE FLAG

by our political correspondent

Observers on all sides of the Atlantic have expressed concern about today's debate in the Atlan Assembly on selling the country to one of three super powers — the United States, the Soviet Union or Western Europe.

Although none of the three superpowers has made any official statement about what their reaction would be if Atlan negotiators knocked on their doors, all three would prefer that the Atlans came to their door and not that of either of the other powers.

Seen from Mid-Atlantic one problem is that much of Atlan has been sold already. Many of the retail and entertainment outlets are owned by United States companies, most of the shipping and air transport is controlled partly or wholly by Soviet commercial interests, and most of the large farms are financed and controlled by the Western Europeans.

Only the oil industry and the gold mines (Atlan is the world's sixteenth largest producer of oil and fifth largest producer of gold) remain in Atlan hands and are completely protected from foreign ownership by Government regulations.

Atlan Television
Television House
Atlan City

MEMO — E.894

From: Editor, NEWSPROBE.

To: Production team, NEWSPROBE, 'Selling the Flag' debate

Since the national audience figures are likely to reach record levels there must be no slip up. Although the actual timing of the slots has not yet been fixed, there will be firm deadlines. If you fail to be ready and there are blank screens then you will be dismissed on the spot. Make a point of being in the studio at least 5 minutes before transmission, and perhaps 10 minutes before.

In view of last week's soggy programme on the environment (see Memo E.891) it is essential that you remember the title of the programme — so probe. Don't ask "What do you feel about the result?" stuff. Go for the nitty gritty — "What happens now?" "What will you personally do about it?" — and so forth.

Do not just reel off a string of questions you have written down. Listen to the replies. Follow up the answers. Probe!!

Part Three
Bibliography

The following list contains some of the better known simulations, plus books and articles on simulations (and some other techniques) related to management, training and education. Details of the professional bodies SAGSET, ISAGA, NASAGA and ABSEL are provided also, at the end of the list.

Brooks G (1987) *Speaking and Listening: Assessment at age 15.* NFER-Nelson: Windsor, UK

Christopher E M and Smith L E (1987) *Leadership Training Through Gaming.* Kogan Page: London, UK/Nichols Publishing: New York, USA

Coote A and McMahon L (1984) Challenging orthodoxy — the use of simulation games in modifying the assumptive worlds of organizational policy makers. In Jaques D and Tipper E (eds) *Learning for the Future with Games and Simulations. Perspectives on Gaming and Simulation 9,* Proceedings of the 1983 SAGSET conference. SAGSET: Loughborough University of Technology, UK

Crookall D, Oxford R, Saunders D (1987) Towards a reconceptualization of simulation: from representation to reality. *Simulation/Games for Learning* 17.4

Davison A and Gordon P (1978) *Games and Simulations in Action.* Woburn Press: London, UK

de-Leon P (1981) The analytic requirements for free-form gaming. *Simulation & Games* 12.2

Duke R D (1974) *Gaming; the Future's Language.* Halsted: New York, USA

Duke R D and Greenblat C S (1979) *Game-generating-games.* Sage: Newbury Park, CA, USA, and London, UK

Duke R D (c1979) METRO-APEX. Published by Environmental Simulation Laboratory, University of Michigan, Ann Arbor, MI 48109, USA

Duke R D and Greenblat C S (1981) *Principles and Practices of Gaming Simulation.* Sage: Newbury Park, CA, USA, and London, UK

Eden C and Fineman S (1986) Problem centred role-play: the challenge of open ended simulation. *Simulation/Games for Learning* 16.1

Elgood C (1984) *Handbook of Management Games* (3rd edn). Gower Press: Aldershot, UK

Ellington H, Addinall E and Percival F (1983) *A Handbook of Game Design*. Kogan Page: London, UK

Faris A J (1987) A survey of the use of business games in academia and business. *Simulation & Games* 18.2

Fisher C W (1975) Value orientations implied or encouraged by METRO-APEX (and some other simulated games) and a suggested change technique. In *Proceedings of the 14th Annual Conference of the North American Simulation and Gaming Association*, University of Southern California Press: Los Angeles, USA

Gooding C and Zimmer T W (1980) Use of specific industry gaming in the selection, orientation and training of managers. *Human Resource Management* 19: 19–23

Goodlad J (1984) *A Place Called School*. McGraw Hill: New York, USA

Goodman F. THEY SHOOT MARBLES, DON'T THEY? Available from NASAGA, Community Systems Foundation, 1130 Hill Street, Ann Arbor, MI 48104-3399, USA

Goodman F. END OF THE LINE. Available from NASAGA, Community Systems Foundation, 1130 Hill Street, Ann Arbor, MI 48104-3399, USA

Greenblat C S (1986) CAPJEFOS: A SIMULATION OF VILLAGE DEVELOPMENT. Available from Cathy Greenblat, Dept Sociology, Rutgers University, New Brunswick, NJ 080903, USA

Greenblat C S (1988) *Designing Games and Simulations*. Sage: Newbury Park, CA, USA, and London, UK

Greenblat C S and Gagnon J H (1975) BLOOD MONEY. National Heart, Lung and Blood Institute, Bethesda: MA, USA

Greenblat C S and Gagnon J H (1981) Further explorations on the multiple reality game. In Greenblat C S and Duke R D (eds) *Principles and Practices of Gaming-Simulation*. Sage: Newbury Park, CA, USA, and London, UK

Hausrath A H (1971) *Venture Simulation in War, Business and Politics*. McGraw-Hill: New York, USA

HM Inspectors of Schools (1988) *The Introduction of the General Certificate of Secondary Education in Schools*. Department of Education and Science: London, UK

Horn R E and Cleaves A (1980) (eds) *The Guide to Simulations/Games for Education and Training*. (4th edn) Sage: Newbury Park, CA., USA, and London, UK

Jamieson I, Miller A, Watts A G (1988) *Mirrors of Work: Work Simulations in Schools.* Falmer Press: London, UK

Jones K (1982) *Simulations in Language Teaching.* Cambridge University Press: Cambridge, UK

Jones K (1984) *Nine Graded Simulations* (SURVIVAL, FRONT PAGE, RADIO COVINGHAM, PROPERTY TRIAL, APPOINTMENTS BOARD, THE DOLPHIN PROJECT, AIRPORT CONTROVERSY, THE AZIM CRISIS, ACTION FOR LIBEL) Max Hueber: Munich. Reprinted under licence under the title *Graded Simulations* (1985) Lingual House/Filmscan: London, UK

Jones K (1987a) *Simulations: A Handbook for Teachers and Trainers* (2nd edn). Kogan Page: London, UK/Nichols Publishing: New York, USA

Jones K (1987b) *Six Simulations* (SPACE CRASH, MASS MEETING, THE RAG TRADE, BANK FRAUD, TELEVISION CORRESPONDENT, THE LINGUAN PRIZE FOR LITERATURE). Basil Blackwell: Oxford, UK

Jones K (1988a) *Interactive Learning Events. A Guide For Facilitators.* Kogan Page: London, UK/Nichols Publishing: New York, USA

Jones K (1988b) Interactive events: national differences in participation and categorisation. In Crookall D, Coote A, Saunders D, Klabbers J H G, Cecchini A, Piane A D (eds) *Simulation-Gaming in Education and Training,* Proceedings of the 1987 ISAGA conference, Venice. Pergamon: Oxford, UK

Jones K (1988c) Why gamesters die in space. In Crookall D, Coote A, Saunders D, Klabbers J H G, Cecchini A, Piane A D (eds) *Simulation-Gaming in Education and Training,* Proceedings of the 1987 ISAGA conference, Venice. Pergamon: Oxford, UK

Jones K (1989) One right and five wrong ways to run simulations. *Topic* (National Foundation for Educational Research journal) Vol.1. 1

Kerr J Y K (1977) Games and simulations in English-language teaching. In *Games, Simulations and Role-playing.* British Council: London, UK

Kuipers H (1983) The role of a game-simulation in a project of change. *Simulation & Games* 14.3

Labov W (1969) *The Logic of Non-standard English.* Center for Applied Linguistics: Washington DC, USA. Also reprinted in Labov, W (1972) *Language in the Inner City.* University of Pennsylvania Press: Philadelphia, USA; also published by Basil Blackwell: Oxford, UK (1977)

Lonergan J (1984) Co-operation, competition, and the individual — some games for beginners. In Jaques D and Tipper E (eds) *Learning for the Future with Games and Simulations. Perspectives on Gaming and Simulation 9.* Proceedings of the 1983 SAGSET conference. SAGSET: Loughborough University of Technology, UK

Mackie D (1986) Simple games for complex situations. In Craig D and Martin A (eds) *Gaming and Simulation for Capability. Perspectives on Gaming and Simulation 11,* Proceedings of the 1985 conference of SAGSET. SAGSET: Loughborough University of Technology, UK

Moses J L (1977) The assessment center method. In Moses J L and Byham W C (eds) *Applying the Assessment Center Method.* Pergamon: Oxford, UK

Moses J L and Byham W C (eds) (1977) *Applying the Assessment Center Method.* Pergamon: Oxford, UK

OSS (1948) *Assessment of Men. Selection of Personnel for the Office of Strategic Services.* Rinehart: New York, USA

Percival F and Ellington H (1988) *A Handbook of Educational Technology: A Practical Guide for Teachers.* Kogan Page: London, UK/Nichols Publishing: New York, USA

Peters T J and Waterman R H (1982) *In Search of Excellence.* Harper and Row: New York, USA

Pfeiffer J W and Jones J E (eds) (1974) *Structured Experiences in Human Relations Training.* Vol. 1. University Associates of Europe: Mansfield, Notts., UK

Pfeiffer J W and Jones J E (eds) (1977) *The 1977 Handbook for Group Facilitators.* University Associates Inc: CA, USA

Powers R B. THE COMMONS GAME. Available from NASAGA, Community Systems Foundation, 1130 Hill Street, Ann Arbor, MI 48104-3399, USA

Radley G (1979) The dynamics of groups in gaming. In Megarry J (ed) *Human Factors in Games and Simulations. Perspectives on Academic Gaming and Simulation 4,* Proceedings of the 1978 SAGSET conference. Kogan Page: London, UK

Rediffusion Simulation Ltd (1986) *Simulation Training — A Guide for Trainers and Managers.* Manpower Services Commission: Sheffield, UK

Ruth L and Murphy S (1988) *Designing Writing Tasks for the Assessment of Writing.* Ablex Publishing: Norwood, NJ, USA

Saunders D M (1985) 'Reluctant participants' in role play simulations: stage fright or bewilderment? *Simulation/Games for Learning.* 15.1

Saunders D M (1986) Drama and simulation: a soap opera game that illustrates dramaturgical perspectives in communication studies. *Simulation & Games* 17.1

Shirts R G (1969) STARPOWER. Simile II: Del Mar, CA, USA

Shirts R G (1977) BAFA BAFA. Simile II: Del Mar, CA, USA

Shirts R G (1977) WHERE DO YOU DRAW THE LINE? Simile II: Del Mar, CA, USA

Stenhouse L (1975) *An Introduction to Curriculum Research and Development.* Heinemann: London, UK

Stradling R et al (1984) *Teaching Controversial Issues.* Arnold: London, UK

Taylor J L and Walford R (1978) *Learning and the Simulation Game.* Open University Press: Milton Keynes, UK

Thatcher D (1983) A consideration of the use of simulation for the promotion of empathy in the training for the caring professions — ME — SLOW LEARNER, a case study. *Simulation/Games for Learning* 13.1

Thatcher D and Robinson J (1986) *ME — SLOW LEARNER.* Solent Simulations: 80 Miller Drive, Fareham, Hants, UK

Van Ments M (1983) 2nd edn 1988 *The Effective Use of Role-Play.* Kogan Page: London, UK/Nichols Publishing: New York, USA

Wittgenstein L (1969). *Philosophical Investigations* (4th edn). Basil Blackwell: Oxford, UK

Bibliography

SAGSET. Society for the Advancement of Games and Simulations in Education and Training. The Society's journal, Simulation/Games for Learning is published quarterly. The proceedings of SAGSET's annual conference, which is usually a series of workshops, are published under the general title Perspectives on Gaming and Simulation. Details from The Secretary, SAGSET, Centre for Extension Studies, University of Technology, Loughborough, Leics LE11 3TU, UK.

ISAGA. International Simulation and Gaming Association. The official journal is Simulation & Games, published quarterly, and available from Sage Publications, Newbury Park, CA 91320, USA and London, UK. There is also *ISAGA Newsletter* available to members only. Secretariat — Jan Klabbers, Department of Social Sciences, PO Box 80.140 3508 TC Utrecht, The Netherlands.

NASAGA. North American Simulation and Gaming Association. Also has *Simulation & Games* as the official journal. Contact – Fred Goodman, Community Systems Foundation, 1130 Hill Street, Ann Arbor, MI 48104-3399, USA

ABSEL. Association for Business Simulation and Experiential Learning. Also has Simulation & Games as the official journal. President — Joseph Wolfe, Department of Management and Marketing, The University of Tulsa, 6000 South College Avenue, Tulsa, OK 74104, USA.